FARM JOURNAL'S
HOUSE PLANTS
FOR
GIFT GIVING

OTHER BOOKS BY THE AUTHORS:

The Indoor Light Gardening Book

Fun with Growing Herbs Indoors

Fun with Growing Odd and
Curious Houseplants

Fun with Terrarium Gardening

Plants that Really Bloom Indoors

The Miracle Houseplants

The House Plant Decorating Book

FARM JOURNAL'S
HOUSE PLANTS
FOR
GIFT GIVING

by VIRGINIE F. and GEORGE A. ELBERT

FARM JOURNAL, INC.
Philadelphia, Pennsylvania

Distributed to the trade by
DOUBLEDAY & COMPANY, INC., Garden City, New York

BOOK DESIGN
Maureen Sweeney

DRAWINGS
John Emil Cymerman

PHOTOS
by the authors

ISBN: 0-385-14005-3

Library of Congress Catalog Card Number 78-60374

DEDICATION

To Ruth E. Buchan
Who has sponsored so many
worthwhile horticultural books

ACKNOWLEDGEMENTS

Photo on page 4 by Douglas M. Crispin, Denver Colorado. All other illustrations by the authors.

We thank the Brooklyn Botanic Garden for permission to photograph its Container Show. The following containers were from the Botanic Garden's shop; pages 11, 21, 43, 92, and 98. Container also supplied by Kitty Bright Designs, page 45.

Other sources of containers were Dallas Trade Mart, N.Y.C., page 18; Dave Grossman Designs, St. Louis, MO., page 15; Goodmans, N.Y.C., page 83; Toscany Imports, N.Y.C., page 80; J. Kenneth Zahn, N.Y.C., page 90. Studios photographed at the Torpedo Factory Art Center, Alexandria, Virginia are those of Nancy Bishop, page 86 and "Going to Pot", page 88.

CAPTIONS FOR FULL-PAGE
BLACK AND WHITE ILLUSTRATIONS

Contents

Exacum affine.

The Joy of Giving Plants

How can one explain the special pleasure associated with the giving of flowers and plants? Observe someone picking out a bouquet or a plant. The choice is dictated almost entirely by personal enjoyment along with an inner vision of the person to whom the present is to be made and of the surroundings in which it is to be displayed. Cost is a consideration, naturally, for everyone has a different budget. But it is rarely the overriding one. Equally rarely do those who receive them value them for their expense.

Golden Cockscomb in a red Venetian glass bowl catches the spirit of Holiday giving.

They have been an expression of love, cheered the ill, graced celebrations and holidays. They have been a message of gratitude for hospitality. Thoughtfulness, good taste or symbolism have given them merit. Where other gifts might be of less value or interest than expected, plants and flowers have never been quite perfunctory. They have invariably introduced into the inescapable sterility of living between walls a touch of the outdoors, of color and of life. In the depths of winter they counteract the gloom like an unexpected harbinger of spring. For lovers they introduce a touch of poetry to the most prosaic of relationships. And in lovers' quarrels they serve as a gesture of reconciliation.

1

Until just a few years ago, these gifts were almost always flowers. A foliage plant was virtually unthinkable. Bouquets were the most popular. Plants were sold in flower for special holidays—pots of tulips, hyacinths or narcissus in bud; azaleas, poinsettias, calceolarias, cinerarias, cyclamen. A gift plant had to be essentially a bouquet with roots. The plants were spectacular, but the list of choices was never very long. They were expected to be temporary like the cut flowers, but lasting somewhat longer. Once their flowers faded, they were simply thrown away. Grown under greenhouse conditions that could not—and still cannot—be duplicated in the home, this was all one *could* do with them.

Now we have gone through a revolution in our attitudes toward plants. The old gift plants we've mentioned continue to be treated as before. But they must compete with an entirely different repertory, correctly called house plants, that have much greater permanence. There

A collector of small art objects will appreciate a group of annual Dianthus plants in silver cups. Or, substitute any other winter-bloomed annuals.

2

are many more long-lasting and more colorful foliage plants than ever before. There are flowering ones that bloom on and off throughout the whole year. Some that are normally short-lived we have learned to propagate so that we need never be without them—a method not possible indoors with the older plants. And, in this same way, we can now multiply our favorite plants and grow our own presents.

The word house plant has gone through a metamorphosis with time. Before the use of artificial light for growing plants, there were two kinds—the flowering gift plants and some very patient foliage plants. Window light was inadequate and heat was unreliable with winter night temperatures dropping to the 40's. It took a tough plant to exist indoors at all.

Nevertheless, there were a few of them that are still with us. The famous Aspidistra, the Cast Iron plant, the Kentia and Parlor palms and Snake plants just about exhausted the possibilities. These were never considered a class apart, but rather were lumped together under the general description of house plants along with the gift plants.

We no longer consider the commercial gift plants as house plants. House plants are flowering and foliage plants that live with us. They've become part of the furnishings of the home. Our garden indoors has become even more a part of our way of life than the outdoor one.

The changes in plants and the indoor environment have taken place over a shorter span of time than the development of cars and airplanes. Thirty-five years might be picked as the outside limit. And these changes also encompass the giving of plants as gifts—the number and kind available, the occasions for giving and even our motivations for choosing them for the purpose.

Fill a red-stained grape basket with Wax Begonias as a birthday centerpiece gift for a girl or boy.

THE CHANGING HOME ENVIRONMENT

It has never been possible to grow northern outdoor perennials in the house because they require freezing temperatures in winter if they are to revive in the spring. Annuals have been considered summer plants, so nobody tried them indoors. But if they had done so, house temperatures in winter would have killed them. The alternative, tropical perennials, also found cold homes intolerable. When heating systems improved and a minimum temperature of 60 degrees F. at night in winter could be sustained, the possibility opened up of growing indoors all the wonderful and rare plants that had been previously seen only in private greenhouses or botanical gardens. Plants growing indoors could be for everybody, rather than just for institutions and the wealthy.

The number of house plants increased considerably, but one element was still lacking—sufficient light. The best place in a house to grow plants was an enclosed sun porch. But it had a ceiling that reduced the hours of bright sunlight so that they did not compensate for long periods of cloudy days. Windows were even more inadequate.

Then, in 1938, the fluorescent lamp was placed on the market and, within a short time, indoor growers discovered that they could use it to supplement sunlight on cloudy days or even grow and bloom plants in dark places by keeping it lighted for longer hours. With the discovery that plants receive their greatest benefit from the red and blue rays of the

Flowering and foliage plants growing under fluorescent light.

spectrum, and when lamps were manufactured to meet these requirements, the era of artificial light gardening was initiated and all tropical
plants became fair game for indoor growing.

In next to no time, people were growing plants where they had never
grown before. The secretary in an inner office could have a green plant
on the desk. A one-room apartment with a window facing the next building could be enlivened with blooming plants growing under a fluorescent
fixture. In a farmhouse enclosed porches, inner rooms and cellars became gardens in winter, rivaling the best of the outdoors in summer. No
longer is gardening seasonal. The winter garden continues the growing
year. Winter plants and flowers are even more desirable than the summer ones that we take for granted.

And plants have become very precious. Gardens, for any number of
reasons, are reduced in size. More people are living in apartment houses
and working in offices without windows. The cities have spread so far
that nature itself is no longer as accessible. But now nature can be
brought indoors and millions have discovered how enchanting it can be.
We have learned to cherish plants as individuals and to treat them as
household pets. More people know more about plants than ever before.

Thus, a tremendous potential market has been created. Nurserymen
tried out plants previously grown only in private greenhouses and botanical gardens and found a public ready to buy them and capable of growing them indoors. Plant explorers brought likely specimens from the
tropics. The ornamental plant departments of our universities helped to
develop new varieties adaptable to indoor growing. Hobbyist amateurs
all over the country had fun trying new plants under artificial light and

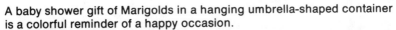

A baby shower gift of Marigolds in a hanging umbrella-shaped container
is a colorful reminder of a happy occasion.

making their own discoveries—later these were grown by nurserymen for sale in shops. Seedsmen also joined the parade, introducing varieties just for house plant growers.

Outdoor gardeners have never bothered to multiply plants. They might divide up large clumps of perennials or collect seed from annual plants. But these were exceptions. Indoor gardeners discovered for themselves that tropical plants were easy to propagate in any quantity they needed. They are now learning that annual plants can be grown and multiplied in winter. Thus, for the first time, any indoor grower is able to produce extra plants for giving. Through giving, indoor gardeners are gaining more and more converts to a love of plants.

Because of the great increase in the number of people growing plants indoors, there has resulted both a rise in the status of plant giving and an enlargement of the list of occasions when they are considered suitable as gifts. Cut flowers and temporary flowering plants have been partly replaced by the more permanent new types of plants.

Decorate the wedding-party table with place markers of small-leaved Fittonia in silvered metal champagne glasses.

As wedding presents we have found plants arouse enthusiasm and gratitude—unthinkable a few years back. A plant is now suitable for a housewarming and is as important, and often as expensive, as a piece of furniture. We can give plants to young people. Not so long ago a girl would have felt short-changed and a boy insulted by a plant gift. Today plants appear on the wish list.

All across the country, year-round benefit sales are held for all kinds of occasions and institutions. Providing saleable objects is an important aspect of national giving for innumerable philanthropic purposes. Here, too, the attitude toward plants has changed with dramatic suddenness. Overnight, the plant sale table has become the mainstay of many worthy organizations and charities. A donation of plants is now recognized as both legitimate and welcome. It is taken for granted that the gift is "homemade," as are so many others, for it is the product of the multiplying zeal of an indoor grower. Benefits have become a large proportion of all gifting.

It is because of all of these recent developments, unique in the long history of giving, that a book on propagating and presenting plants becomes timely. The majority of amateurs have only a few kinds. Here we propose to tell you about many more that you will discover are appropriate gifts that you can grow in the house and can multiply for every occasion. We trust that you will find new ideas, more beautiful plants and both practical and attractive ways of presenting them. It is one of the greatest good fortunes of life to be able to give, and the wonderful repertory of house plants will, we believe, enhance your pleasure.

8   Episcia.

Persons and Occasions for Plant Giving

As we've already pointed out, plant giving has much wider acceptance than formerly. Deciding what kind of plant will be most acceptable is a simple matter if your gift is for a member of the family or an intimate friend. But what if it is for an acquaintance or, as in benefit sales, for complete strangers? Then it helps to be jogged on the category of plant that would be most appropriate. Propagation takes time. If you can plan ahead for your gift needs, you will be ready with the right plant and the right container. So, in the next few pages, we'll remind you of the many situations where plants fit the person or the occasion.

BEGINNER and INEXPERIENCED GROWER

We usually give plants to those who have some already, and shy away from taking the risk with people who have never grown before. It seems obvious that the gift would be unwelcome and we conclude that a friend or relative is far too busy to care for a plant. If we know that some person has another hobby, we'll guess that it will be hard to arouse interest in a new one. There are also all those people who have no hobbies, are in a rut, think learning anything new is too much effort, and generally cut themselves off from everything but their routine activities.

However, we have learned that plants are very seductive indeed. Once you are brought into contact with them, you will find them difficult to resist. So many are very undemanding, yet have definite personalities. Time and again, we have seen hobbyless people become absolutely enchanted by a plant gift—soon they are very much concerned with its well-being. Now that indoor gardening is a popular hobby, no one need feel self-conscious about drooling over plants.

Lots of city people grow up entirely ignorant of the operations of nature. We have known some who were visibly shocked at the suggestion that plants need food—as if they grew spontaneously out of the soil. So, when choosing a plant for a beginner, take little for granted. The plant must be one of the very easiest, such as *Oxalis regnellii*. It will be very helpful if you take the trouble to write out instructions for the plant's care. New city growers want absolute rules, for they tend to think of a plant as no different than a typewriter and they expect effect to follow cause just like a machine. Yet we have seen city folk with just such a lack of basic knowledge who, once given a plant, learn more about it in one year than many outdoor gardeners do in a lifetime. The plant is not outside in the garden—it lives indoors where it can't be ignored. Really busy people, we've noticed, are usually very good with plants. It is the disorganized ones, swooning over plants, who make a mess of them.

Young people, who have to begin some time, are therefore also in this category, but they are a special case and we discuss them separately.

As for the people who have had only a short experience with plants, there is every reason to make them such presents, for they are in the process of expanding their collections and will be grateful for almost any addition. Give them the simpler plants they don't yet own.

INTERMEDIATE GROWER

There are many amateurs who have a variety of plants and sufficient interest to experiment with more difficult ones. But, until they become really knowledgeable, they remain intermediate growers. So, intermediate may describe an amateur on the way to becoming an expert or one who may never advance beyond a modest competence.

What really separates the expert from the intermediate grower is the former's ability to organize long experience with plants so that observation of their condition is almost automatic and discovering an appropriate solution to difficulties is normal. Intermediate growers, on the other hand, have to treat each case by itself. They ask questions or refer to books, and may or may not arrive at proper culture, depending not on their own knowledge but on what can be derived from others. This makes a big difference in the kinds of plants you can give an intermediate. But at least the intermediate grower already has *some* experience and will appreciate and take better care of a more sophisticated plant, such as Lobelia, than a beginner. A very common plant will not suit this class of grower who has already been through Coleus, Spider Plants, Swedish Ivy, *Tradescantia* and the like.

EXPERT GROWER

Any indoor grower who can keep a varied collection of flowering and foliage plants in good shape can be judged an expert. A degree in horticulture or special knowledge of botany is unnecessary. Many amateurs we know have more practical skill in handling the indoor plant repertory than professors of horticulture.

Knowing which plants are in an expert's collection is a pre-condition to choosing a suitable present. Search among your own plants for one that he or she is missing. It need not be a great rarity, but certainly shouldn't be a common plant. *Pereskia aculeata* var. *godseffiana* is a possibility. Pothos is not. An attractive novelty will probably be a sure-fire success. Groom the plant carefully; experts appreciate neat growth.

Experts are in some respects easier to please than intermediate growers. They are often less opinionated, less inclined to fuss over technicalities, and less concerned with displaying their superior knowledge. A good plant, and one that they do not have, will be accepted in the spirit with which it is given.

Mail-order catalogs and variety nurserymen have numerous plants that are not just run-of-the-mill. Keep a few handy to propagate for your more knowledgeable grower friends and acquaintances. In spite of its simplicity, our cultural plant list includes a number of items that should be of interest to any expert you know.

An unknown species, such as *Crassula* Sp. *Barrydale,* is a safe bet for an expert. Such plants are often found at large nurseries. The unusual molded clay container enhances the plant.

Kohleria 'Rongo' well-grown is gorgeous. All these plants and other expert choices can be bought from the special nurseries that grow them; then propagate for gifts.

SPECIAL PLANT HOBBYIST

The special plant hobbyist is easy to identify in the horticultural community—someone who grows just one kind of plant almost exclusively, and is almost always an active member of a society with the same interest. Examples of these plant interests are Gesneriads, African Violets, Begonias, Orchids, Cacti, Bromeliads, Fuchsias, Ferns, Ivies, and Geraniums. Hobbyists are experienced growers, but not necessarily expert except in their own specialty. They may know next to nothing about indoor growing in general, but be whizzes at growing that one plant.

The special plant hobbyist is a difficult person to please. The specialist is not interested in other plants and usually has very definite opinions about the relative values of plants. Don't dare venture on your own judgement to give one for the collection. The only way to overcome this stumbling block is to consult another specialist as to the latest novelty that your friend does not possess or some rarity that he is seeking. That leaves little room for propagation unless you have several such friends. The one rare exception is if you happen to have a very unusual African Violet, Begonia or Geranium, as the case may be. But it is difficult to overestimate the critical faculties of a specialty plant hobbyist. It is often better to give something other than a plant.

In our listing we will try to suggest a few plants that might assuage the savage beast.

The gesneriads, African Violet relatives, include many plants that will please an expert. This *Drymonia stenophylla* will bloom every day indoors.

Sinningia cardinalis is usually red. This one is white. An expert will love it.

A new hybrid like this *Columnea* 'Red King' makes a special gift for the expert grower.

CHILDREN and YOUNG PEOPLE

Accustoming children to plants should start early, for later on it can be more difficult to train them to the routines of care. In our experience, when children see their parents growing plants indoors, they consider this part of a normal household and look forward to sharing this adult activity. What can kill the sense of participation is an overdose of parental fussiness and discipline.

Plants must be given, not loaned. The child must have a sense of ownership from the start. All that is really required for minimum care is a little watering can, so see that the child has one. Tell the child what the plant needs with an occasional reminder—but don't nag. It does no harm to help with a watering which has been neglected or to let the child know that you have done so because the plant "looked bad." But don't make this a serious offense. One slip of this kind can spoil everything.

The best plants for a child are small ones that need minimum attention. *Oxalis regnellii* is an excellent choice and so are Spider Plants and *Kalanchoe tubifloras* because of their way of growing plantlets. Trailing *Ficus*, Pothos or one of the *Tradescantia* group are all reliable. The Prayer Plant needs a bit more care but is still a good possibility.

14

The funniest animal pots we've ever seen. Any kid will love them filled with Wax Begonias, *Oxalis regnellii* or Wandering Jew.

This Wandering Jew, *Tradescantia albiflora* 'albovittata', is easy to grow and showy for the window of a child's room.

Even if they come from plantless families, adolescent boys and girls are still influenced by their peers, among whom plant growing is enormously popular. They are imitative and will want plants of the kinds possessed by their friends. Follow their lead, not your own preferences, and you can't go wrong.

A serious oversight is committed if you give only the plant. Don't forget to provide a watering can, a saucer and a package of fertilizer. If these are missing, the chances are good that by the time the young person has provided these accessories, the plant will be dead.

Do not fear to give a young man a plant. If you are of the generation in which a boy growing ornamental plants for pleasure was considered sissy, you don't have to worry any longer. Male collegiate dormitories are full of plants.

HOLIDAYS

The most traditional plant gift situations are holidays. The whole florist industry plans for those unique occasions, Christmas and Easter, when it seems that the entire country invades the flower shops. To meet this mass market, there are mass plants—Kalanchoes and Poinsettias at Christmas, bulb plants and Azaleas at Easter. The same plants are repeated with deadly regularity year after year. You can do a real service by surprising someone with your own, different plant.

For Christmas there are plenty of red-colored plants—if you must give red. Consider Coleus, Crape Myrtle, Crown of Thorns and African Violets for starters. Or a change in color will be welcomed. Holiday gift

For a holiday, what about a cow creamer planted with rosemary? Or, give a whole coffee set with appropriate plants. Perhaps a cut glass sugar as both pot and gift?

plants are impermanent. A house plant is for keeps.

Another great plant-giving occasion is Mother's Day when Sweetheart Roses are in the ascendancy, Azaleas are still going strong and Cyclamen, Cinerarias, Calceolarias and Gloxinias can be considered. Or, try an herb for the kitchen.

As for papa, the florists haven't made a serious play for Father's Day business. He gets a tie he doesn't want or a razor to replace the old one he prefers. You can't do worse with a plant. Nowadays he won't be insulted, because there are plenty of other fathers around who enjoy indoor growing. By and large, you will please him best not so much with a beautiful plant as with an odd one. Try an Oxalis or Pea family plant that closes its leaves at night or a *Kalanchoe* that produces plantlets on the leaves.

BIRTHDAYS, ANNIVERSARIES and RETIREMENTS

We group these three occasions together because they are important and a casual present just won't do. But they have the advantage of being known dates so that you can start propagating plants well ahead of time.

We have already said that it is quite proper to give a plant to a begin-

Small or large Ming Aralias are useful and long-lasting gifts.

ner. But to do so on a major occasion when the person expects a gift that is either really useful or that contributes to other interests or hobbies is to court disaster. We can only suggest plants for these events if the person involved is a true plant lover. By careful inquiry, you may find out their plant preferences. Every indoor gardener has such desires—plants that they would like to own but have not had the opportunity or means to acquire.

Someone who has been growing only in a window would appreciate plants and a fluorescent lighting unit. When a really sumptuous gift is in order, friends might pool their efforts and provide a complete indoor garden. Retirement is a fine time for such a project.

A Norfolk Island Pine, *Araucaria excelsa,* in an easily movable pot is a gift of a lifetime. The casters are very convenient since this grows into a good-sized indoor tree.

HOSTESS PRESENTS

Hostess or hospitality presents are usually modest and all we are doing here is proposing the substitution of a homegrown plant for the traditional box of candy or bouquet. A plant is a more personal gift—quite different from the usual hostess present. It is more long-lasting and usually bears a story. No one who grows indoors just hands over such a different or unusual gift. How the plant was acquired, the problems with it and its culture are always subjects of conversation.

We suggest giving young plants of easy culture in attractive containers. Large size is not necessarily a merit since the host or hostess may have limited space for growing indoors. A nice touch is to help find a suitable and attractive location for the plant.

A coffee mug decorated with an herbal design makes a fine pot for *Lavandula dentata*. A useful and decorative hostess present. The herb is sweetly perfumed.

Rosemary—for remembrance—is a friendship gift
at a farewell party.

SHOWER GIFTS

Showers are a chance for friends of the bride to present a sort of trousseau consisting of useful, relatively inexpensive presents. They often have a theme—gifts for the kitchen, the bedroom, the dining room. Sometimes they are labelled miscellaneous. Herbs are a natural choice for the kitchen. A palm or a succulent will look well in a bedroom and will demand little attention. For the dining table, one or more plants in a decorative container, meant for a centerpiece, is appropriate.

Friends arranging the shower can add a nice touch to the table by having a small gift for the bride's guests as a place marker. Small plants set in silver-plated cups can be altogether decorative. How about "Rosemary for remembrance?"

WEDDINGS

It is rather difficult to think of the right plant for a wedding present. But, when you consider the duplication of salad bowls, blenders and mixers, almost anything different has a chance of being appreciated. One problem is that young people are usually too busy right after the ceremony, and too wrapped up in each other, to take care of a plant properly. If the newlyweds are ardent plant lovers, you can take the chance. You might buy an expensive and unusual plant. But to think of growing it yourself from a cutting or seed requires a degree of prophetic foresight worthy of Nostradamus.

We have given a plant wedding present just once. Our dear friends grew orchids. Another orchid would not have been sensational and might have run counter to their tastes. Instead, we bought them a large specimen of a rare succulent that was also extraordinary in appearance. They were enchanted and preferred it to any other gift they received. That worked fine, but it was a bought plant, not homegrown.

There are situations, though exceptional, where giving your own plant will be proper. You might have brought a propagated plant on to sub-

What a wedding present! *Pittosporum tobira variegata* beautifully grown and a classically designed square pot.

stantial size and beauty that you know will look well in a couple's new home. Or, the young folk may have at some time admired one of your plants. Propagate it or, if it will not break your heart, give the very plant they have admired.

PARTY GIFTS and FAVORS

People would certainly use plants more for party gifts if they knew how to go about buying or producing them. That is what this book is all about. When you compare the value and appeal of a plant at each place setting with the customary stereotyped commercial junk, its superiority is evident—a difference between make-believe satisfaction and real pleasure. You can multiply and pack plants yourself with ease and at virtually no cost, whereas conventional gifts always seem to involve skimping. In addition, the little plants will be a decoration for the table.

The kinds of plants used should be easy to propagate, reasonably fast-growing and showy at an early stage. Blooming Marigolds look splendid on a Thanksgiving table, and other annuals on our list will fit a variety of occasions.

What more charming favor than a silver sugar bowl cache-pot with a little plant for each guest?

PLANTS for the ILL or HOSPITALIZED

It is a very ancient myth that plants are unhealthy in a bedroom or a sick room. The theory has been that they absorb oxygen from the air, with the implication that you can be at least partly asphyxiated in your bed. This happens to be the reverse of the truth, because plants absorb carbon dioxide and give out oxygen. If anything, they improve the quality of the air.

But, to a limited extent, we must be careful about plants given to the ill. The adverse effects are due to odors and pollens. That is why flowers are often taken out of hospital rooms by nurses. And, for this reason, all plants should be without bloom or under cover if they are to live temporarily in a sick room.

For a person who is going to be in a hospital for only a few days, or for one who is chronically ill at home but quite capable of and interested in taking care of plants, there is wide latitude in the choice. But when incapacitation is prolonged, the only plants to be considered are those that can go without attention for long periods of time. This is made possible by giving plants in terrariums. A single fern, a miniature African Violet, *Fittonia* or *Ficus* in a small jar makes a cheerful gift.

We cannot recommend spiny cactus as a plant that needs little care, because of the risk of touching it. But succulents, especially those with a long dormant period, are fine. We suggest Gasterias, some of the Euphorbias, Sansevierias, Cissus (desert kinds), and Haworthias. Nurseries that specialize in succulents can supply you with excellent plants that will exactly fill the bill. However, since not everyone is a succulent enthusiast, a terrarium gift is your best bet.

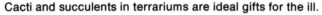

Cacti and succulents in terrariums are ideal gifts for the ill.

PLANTS for BENEFITS

Benefit sales are among the most important sources of revenue for all kinds of non-profit and philanthropic organizations, from plant societies to hospitals to churches to PTAs. They take place throughout the year, all over the country, and usually are dependent upon innumerable relatively small donations. We are all familiar with the immense activity that goes on in baking cakes, making candies, crocheting and knitting. Many people who are unable to give money to their favorite charities are able to contribute in this way. Plants are a new element in this picture and have recently been very popular and successful.

Indoor gardeners have been principal donors to these sales. They have started plants from seed or cuttings well ahead of time. We have done this and have been able to provide an organization with as many as 100 plants in a month, growing them in quite a small amount of space. That does not mean that we produced such quantities in a month—we kept the plants coming along at all times and, whenever we had plants from which we could take cuttings, started new ones.

Most of the small plants were in 2-inch pots. But, inevitably, we and other amateurs had larger plants that were either salable at a higher

Many of our examples, among which are herbs Lavender *dentata*, basil and rosemary, are just right for the benefit table or raffle, attracting more buyers at higher prices.

price or were put into a raffle or auction. Naturally all the proceeds of such sales went to the society treasury.

Because of the personal involvement and the service to a worthy cause, this is one of the most satisfactory kinds of giving. Selecting plants and seed that have the greatest appeal at the sale table introduces you to many varieties that you might not otherwise have thought of growing.

The preparation of plants can be done on an individual basis or as an organized effort. Societies with resale numbers can buy seedlings or partly grown plants from nurseries in quantity at very low wholesale prices. These can be distributed to a committee that grows them to sale-table size. Seed can be bought and distributed in the same way. When large numbers of a desirable plant are not available, mature ones can be bought and used to supply cutting material to members of the committee who then root the cuttings and grow the plants to a proper size.

Proper size, even in the smallest pots, is important. Too often, propagator-donors deliver cuttings that are not well rooted or seedlings that have not yet developed the strength to survive a change in environment. It takes patience to grow plants to the point where they can be safely taken home and grown further. If you intend to give plants, make up your mind that these will be well grown, rather than a perfunctory donation.

The value of plants at the benefit sale table is greatly enhanced by clean, neat or decorative potting. We emphasize the package for any plant gift. And that package is inevitably the pot or a suitable cache-pot. Many plants are colorful and decorative in themselves. But the majority, especially as juveniles, gain greatly when they are in a container that is properly proportioned and gives the plant a proper frame. Dressing plants is much like dressing ourselves. We know very well the difference made in our appearance depending upon whether we are wearing work suits or dresses or those that we don for pure adornment. The plant, too, gains from pretty clothing.

Grooming is also important. Each plant should be carefully trimmed, and all dead leaves and branch ends should be removed. The soil should be carefully smoothed and, preferably, covered with pebbles to make a background for stems and leaves.

In short, giving for benefit sales can be a wonderful exercise in growing and in making the plants look their best. You will be making a donation of greatest value. Your involvement and concern will be made apparent by the appearance of your plants.

26

Buying
Seeds and Plants

The main purpose of this book is to suggest ways of multiplying plants for gifts. Of course you have to start with either seeds or plants. Seed is, in most instances, the more difficult way to go about it indoors, but it is by far the most economical. For this reason alone, we wish that we could have listed only those plants for which seeds are available.

Unfortunately, though there are innumerable seed dealers supplying by mail order to retail customers, their lists, with few exceptions, consist of garden flowers and vegetables. For an outdoor garden, relatively large amounts of seed are required because we plant them not separately but in masses. The indoor gardener, on the contrary, needs only a few plants at one time. Thus, the demand is small. There are a number of large wholesale seed dealers catering to the indoor plant nursery trade, but very few who supply the retail grower.

The whole difficulty is compounded by the relative scarcity of tropical seeds of ornamentals which are often collected in the wild. In our source list we name the major retail suppliers, but we must warn that some of the choicest items are only occasionally available and must be bought when the opportunity offers.

Garden clubs and plant societies can buy wholesale, and this is a convenient means for members to receive seeds of scarce items. The organization can buy large packets, repack the seeds and charge enough for a profit. Not only will the members gain, but the organization can earn income. It is surprising that this is not done by more societies or organizations.

Seedsmen who specialize in tropical ornamentals are quite reliable because most of their business is with nurseries that demand quality. A problem is created for the buyer primarily by the nature of the seed itself. Some tropical ornamental seed germinates as quickly as annual seed. But there are many kinds that belong to two more difficult categories: seed that must be shipped and planted very quickly before it loses its viability, and seed that takes a very long time to germinate.

Quick-germinating seed is soft and grows as soon as it is dropped to the ground. It must be shipped immediately it is ripe, often in special, slightly moistened bags and soil. As soon as it arrives, it must be planted. Such seed is sensitive to low temperatures during shipment and requires special handling. Seedsmen take every precaution, but accidents sometimes do happen. When you are ordering tropical seed, always ask the seedsman to give you prior notice of quick-germinating seed and the approximate date that it will be shipped. None of the plants we list are in this category, but there are so many others you will want to try that this advice may be useful in the future.

The more common type of seed is slow germinating, taking weeks or even months. *Lantana* is very slow and *Crossandra* moderately so. Bushy or tree plants often have very hard-shelled seeds that take from a month to more than a year to germinate. During that time they must be kept moist. A favorite way of speeding up germination is to file a small area on the side of the seeds—never the tips—down to the flesh, then soak overnight in water before planting. Bean family and palm seeds are of this type.

Provided seed is available, you should be able to propagate any of your own plants this way. However, remember that some of the most popular ones are either hybrids or have variegated leaves. Even if you can produce seeds, the new plants will not be the same as the parents. Only vegetative propagation supplies a plant that is the mirror image of the parent. This also applies to many novelty annuals, if they produce seed at all.

Whenever it is possible, we prefer vegetative propagation indoors. It does involve purchasing plants in the first place. But it is faster and more reliable and this is not much of a problem, for in the normal process of trimming and grooming, cuttings can be made. Organizations can buy large plants, assign members to care for them and make arrangements that they be trimmed regularly and the cuttings distributed. When benefit sale tables are a regular feature of fund raising, this method rapidly pays off the original plant and returns a profit.

Whenever it is possible, buy plants from a local florist or nursery. Usually country nurseries are less expensive than city shops.

Any place that retails plants has some that have been shipped from suppliers and are moved out as fast as possible. They have a newly potted look and growth is often weak. Other plants may have been living in the greenhouse or shop for some time. These have a settled look, and have been tested in the environment. The latter are the safer plants.

If you are buying the plant to give away, a neat and compact appearance is preferable. But plants bought with the idea of propagating are better for this purpose if they are well-branched and have been somewhat overgrown. You can trim such plants, use the cuttings, and still end up with a neat specimen. The active growth also is evidence of the vigor of the plant.

Check the kind of soil used in the pot. If it is ordinary garden soil or black bottom soil you know that you will have to repot in soilless mix. If the soil is porous and organic, chances are that you will not have to disturb the plant.

Examine the undersides of leaves and the lower stems and branches for insects. It is surprising how few people look at a plant closely when they are buying. Later they discover an infestation but have no recourse to the seller. Look especially for scale, mite and mealybug. Water the soil before the plant is packed. If there are soil insects or slugs, they'll come promptly to the top.

A solid clay or plastic pot is fine, but beware of very lightweight nursery growth pots, usually plastic, unless you are prepared to repot in something more sturdy.

If the plant is bought in a very hot greenhouse or shop, or in a shop with intensely cool air conditioning (often the case in chain groceries handling plants), consider the environment to which it is to be moved. Any sudden move from hot to cool or cool to hot is damaging to tropical plants. This is the main reason why so many plants suddenly lose leaves or become infected when they have been in the house for a short time. If the shop has been hot, be careful to place your plant in a warm environment at home, if only temporarily, and gradually accustom it to any coolness it will have to endure on a day-to-day basis. The same principle applies if you are moving the plant from a cool to a warm house.

All changes of environment are a shock to plants. Be very careful about watering in the first weeks. Give rather less moisture than normal for that plant. If it starts to grow actively, that is a sign that you can water freely. But if it is semi-dormant after the change of place, don't soak the soil completely.

Many plants useful for gifts and for propagating but rare in shops can be bought through mail order. The specialist nurseries are rarely mass producers and their products are not seen on the market. Many of these potentially valuable plants are not listed here because they are not universally available at any time of the year. But you will want to experiment, and mail-order houses are your best sources.

Transporting plants by mail or United Parcel is a ticklish matter. Nurserymen all have different packings, some more, some less successful. Plants are offered in pots and bare root, depending upon the type. Most nurseries will not ship tropical material in winter. You will have to anticipate your winter needs and order in summer. Ask the nurseryman to ship in summer during a cool spell. Enclosed in their packing, the plants will go to pieces if shipped in a heat wave for any great distance.

Mail shipments should be delivered immediately. If you expect a package and have to be absent from your home, warn the post office and make arrangements with a neighbor. A day of delay may ruin your plants.

As soon as the shipment is received, unpack it carefully and pot up the plants immediately. If there is damage, report it to the shipper promptly.

Not all mail-order houses make restitution, which is one of the hazards of ordering in this way, but some will replace plants.

Not all nurseries are good shippers. In our source list we have been selective, but we cannot avoid shippers with unusually fine collections but relatively poor packing methods. When trying a shipper, start with a small order first before committing yourself to an expensive shipment.

In the following chapter, we will give you more specific cultural directions for starting plants, whether from seed or from plants that you have bought for your own enjoyment and from which you take cuttings to be rooted for gifts.

Very Simple Culture

Over the last few years, indoor gardeners have learned that they can grow most plants by following a few simple rules and formulas. They can be summed up as follows:

1. Provide a very porous soil with good water retention.
2. Give sufficient light according to the needs of each plant.
3. Keep most plants evenly moist.
4. Fertilize regularly with mild solutions.
5. Don't let the temperature drop below 55 degrees F. for some foliage plants or 65 degrees F. for other foliage plants and all flowering plants.

Let's take a look at each of these.

SOIL

Most indoor gardeners use soilless mixes consisting of sphagnum peat moss, vermiculite and perlite. Each of these materials can be bought in packages at all kinds of stores that carry indoor gardening materials. There are four formulas which are known by their proportions of the components we've named.

1-1-1	2-1-1	3-2-1	1-1-2	
1	2	3	1	sphagnum peat moss
1	1	2	1	vermiculite
1	1	1	2	perlite

Components of a soilless mix clockwise from the left—perlite, vermiculite, peat moss. Crushed eggshell in the center.

Each number represents parts of the mix. 3-2-1, therefore, is 3 parts sphagnum peat moss, 2 parts vermiculite and 1 part perlite. When we come to describing the different gift plants, we will use only the formula numbers.

A good soil can also be made by employing sterilized garden soil. It is about equivalent to 2-1-1 soilless mix.

> 1 part sterilized garden soil
> 1 part humus
> 1 part sphagnum peat moss
> 1 part perlite

Finally, there are a few plants, not succulents, that prefer a quick-drying, rather hard soil.

> 3 parts sterilized garden soil
> 1 part perlite

The ingredients are usually mixed dry and then water is added.

Peat moss has an acid reaction that increases the more it is fertilized and watered. In areas that have soft water, we add lime to counteract the acidity. The best form is dolomite lime chips or eggshells. The lime chips come in packages. As for the eggshells, save them from breakfast, dry them for a couple of days and then either spin them in a blender or break them up with a pestle and mortar.

LIGHT

DAYLIGHT

A three-sided sun room or porch with open exposures to the east, west and south receives about one third as much sunlight as a greenhouse. Windows receive much less, for even with a southern exposure, full sun lasts only a few hours. In summer, daylight is brighter but the sun is so high in the sky that only plants near the window receive it directly. In winter, when the sun is lower, its direct rays last longer but there are also longer spells of cloudy weather and temperature and humidity are lower.

In any calculation of the effect of sunlight, city dwellers must reckon with the effects of pollution, not only on the intensity of the light but on the ability of plants to absorb it. A 30 percent reduction in efficiency is a rough guess.

At the window sill there is a period of Full Sun. Further back into the room, at most 2 or 3 feet, is a zone of Partial Sun. Beyond that are zones of Bright Reflected light and Light Shade. The light requirements of plants can be approximately rated in these terms. Many of our best foliage plants can manage with Bright Reflected or Light Shade. All the flowering plants require Partial or Full Sun, with perhaps one unique exception—*Oxalis regnellii*.

With some foliage plants, Light Shade is sufficient. But if the plants you want to grow demand more light, you must supplement daylight with several hours of additional light from fluorescent lamps or the Wonderlite. (See Artificial Light.) If you want to bloom plants by daylight, you must have them close to the window sill. And, even then, you will be able to count on flowering only in spring and summer. At least 5 hours of supplemental artificial light on bright days and 8 to 10 hours on dull ones will be needed to keep plants blooming through the winter.

The implication of this information is that foliage plants can usually be grown throughout the year indoors in Light Shade to Bright Reflected light. But if you wish to grow in shade, you must use artificial light. As for flowering plants, they can be bloomed away from a sunny window only with the aid of artificial light. With all the improvements in home environments for plants, artificial light proves to be the one source of light that is effective.

Inevitably this means that, in describing our gift plants, we must mention the artificial light requirements when the plants are of a type that fit in a light garden at all. For the same reasons, anyone who wants to propagate gifts will be handicapped if only window light is available. Having a fluorescent light unit is very nearly a necessity and definitely a convenience if you want to do much propagating.

ARTIFICIAL LIGHT

In addition to daylight, we can now grow entirely by artificial light. The great advantage of artificial light is that it is available every day of the year. By longer hours of use, we compensate for the lack of intensity compared with daylight. Ten hours per day is sufficient for many of the foliage plants. Flowering plants require 12 hours a day in summer and 14 to 16 hours in winter.

There are only two sources of artificial light that we can use indoors effectively for growing and flowering plants. One is the fluorescent tube. It is also the most economical lamp, producing 3 to 4 times as much light useful to plants per watt than an incandescent bulb, and lasting 10 times longer or more. The only good growth bulb, in our opinion, is the Wonderlite, which we will discuss below.

At a time when a decline in energy use becomes advisable and when energy costs rise, the fluorescent lamp offers a reasonable solution. Those who hesitate to install these lamps should consider that they can have a dual purpose, since they can be used for general lighting and for reading at the very same time that they are growing plants. By combining these uses, you can avoid any substantial increase in your use of energy and in your lighting bills. As an example, a 20-watt tube can easily replace a 100-watt bulb for reading.

Fluorescent fixtures and tubes. The standard fluorescent fixture has two tubes, each 20 watts, 24 inches long or two 40-watt tubes, 48 inches long with reflector. Throughout our plant descriptions, when we recommend the placing of plants closer or farther away from the tubes, the units we have in mind are these. They are available in commercial models, white enameled, for hanging, in table models with stands, and in ceiling fixtures of various designs. The least expensive model is in the $10-$12 range without stand and the $23-$29 range with it. This relatively small investment puts you in business for gift propagating throughout the year.

In theory, these fixtures deliver a maximum of 800 foot-candles to the plants when the lamps are new. In practice, we rate them at 500 foot-candles maximum, but this is sufficient for any growing chore. Foliage plants can be grown with their tops as far away as 2 feet. Flowering plants are often kept with their tops just 3 to 4 inches below the tubes. The maximum range is about 15 inches, depending upon the plant's need for light and the humidity in the environment. The higher the humidity, the less light is needed. Plants in terrariums need less light than those out in the room. In regard to economy, note that even the larger fixtures use only 80 watts compared with a normal 75- or 100-watt incandescent reading lamp that covers a much smaller area.

The fixtures consist of a box in two parts containing the ballast and lamp sockets at either end. They can be screwed to the underside of a shelf or hung from cup hooks. By means of a light chain, they can be made adjustable. Most of the standing models are adjustable on their standards.

There has been complaint that these fixtures are ugly. They need not be. By painting them the same color as your wall, you can make them virtually invisible. So-called strip fixtures without reflectors can be screwed onto the bottoms of shelves and the shelf itself can be used as a reflector by painting with flat white. Enamel and mirror, in spite of appearances, are less reflective. If you doubt our word, consult any lighting expert and you will receive confirmation.

Advanced growers have bigger fixtures with more than two tubes. These are usually set 4 to 6 inches apart measured from the centers of the tubes. A hobbyist may have 12 or more tubes in a row. This increases the intensity somewhat and also side-lights the plants more effectively, producing more compact growth.

In a given shelving space, the tubes do not have to stretch the whole distance and fit closely in the space. Twenty-four-inch tubes can be used in a 36-inch space and 48-inch tubes for a 60-inch space. The excess space at the ends is useful for propagation, for low-light foliage plants, and for resting plants. This arrangement results in a more effective and economical use of the lights.

The 24- and 48-inch tubes are the most efficient ones made, primarily because they are produced in the greatest number. There are a number of other lengths to fit special situations but, without exception, they are more expensive and less economical in operation. You will be surprised to discover that even a 24-inch tube is more expensive than a 48-incher. This is due to a difference in the volume of sales.

Just as incandescent lamps start to dim long before they blow out, fluorescent lamps also deteriorate, although at a slower pace. Because the growth spectrum is the first to suffer, it is advisable to change lamps every 1½ years if you are growing plants requiring a high intensity of light. Otherwise, you can let lamps run until they go off of their own accord. Efficiency can be increased by wiping off your tubes with a damp rag every month or so. The loss of light through dust accumulation is much larger than you might think.

The reason for the need of a reflective surface is that the tube gives out as much light upward away from the plants as downward. So, it is important to reflect as much of that light onto the plants as possible.

We do not recommend the new unit, tube-and-fixture, throw-away models. Efficiency, in our opinion, is very low, useful life is much shorter and this, with the extra expense of a fixture that is not permanent, means a considerable increase in cost without any compensatory feature except that you do not have to screw in the tubes.

Nor do we recommend most of the so-called "growth lamps," not only because some are inefficient, but even more because the color of the light in most instances is unbearable in the home unless it is stuck in a cellar or workroom environment.

We *do* favor the use of Warm White and Cool White tubes. They are the cheapest, most commonly used commercial lamps and the most efficient producers of light. Long ago, amateurs discovered their effectiveness in growing and blooming plants, and very recently the U.S. Department of Agriculture has finally come to the same conclusion. In a two-tube fixture, use *one of each.* In fixtures with a greater number of tubes, *alternate* them.

The other outstanding tube is Verilux TruBloom, sold by Verilux Inc., of 35 Mason Street, Greenwich, Conn. 06830, by mail order. This one tube does the job even better than the combination of Cool and Warm White. The light is excellent for both foliage and blooming plants. It is particularly effective in maintaining compact growth and improving bloom color. The illumination is non-glaring and restful. It is the only tube, in our opinion, that provides daylight color and is tolerable in living areas.

Fluorescent light is your best bet for growing small foliage and flowering plants. In this sense it is a space-saver, for you can crowd small plants for gifts under units fitted one on top of each other, as in shelving.

Reflector bulbs. There are many types of reflector lamps on the market that are used for lighting and display in stores, showrooms, lobbies, etc. A reflector lamp is one that has a reflector inside the bulb itself. Standard R lamps, or incandescent reflector bulbs, that screw into normal ceramic sockets (required for all high-wattage reflector lamps), produce considerable heat damaging to plants and are wasteful of electricity, but will maintain large low-light foliage plants if placed at least 1½ feet above their tops.

We want to warn readers regarding the small reflector bulbs sold in variety and other stores as plant maintenance lamps. These, in our opinion, are nothing more than very poor incandescent lamps at a high price. The heat output is terrific, the light output is low, and their life expectancy is very poor. A rank beginner who has been told that more light is needed for plants will naturally gravitate toward anything called a Plant Bulb, expecting it to perform wonders. Hence the market success of lamps that have little or no merit.

The one lamp that is outstanding is of very recent development. It is called Wonderlite and is manufactured by the Public Service Lamp Corp. of 410 West 16th Street, New York, N.Y. 10011. It is a 160-watt mercury-vapor reflector lamp that screws into a normal *ceramic* socket. The socket is the same size as you use for an incandescent house bulb and ceramic sockets are on sale at any store carrying electrical supplies.

The Wonderlite utilizes a new substance called Phosphorsol to provide a balanced growth spectrum and a good daylight color that is compatible with your incandescent household lighting and does not distort natural colors. It is the first lamp of this type capable of blooming plants. Although the initial expense is high (in the $30-40 range), it covers as much area as four 48-inch fluorescent tubes which, with fixture and reflector, will cost at least the same. It lasts 12,000 hours compared with less than 1,000 hours for a standard R lamp.

This lamp can be used on a ceiling track, clamped to a pole or fitted into a standing lamp. It is, therefore, the latest and best solution for growing big ornamental plants that cannot be handled with fluorescent fixtures. It can light gardens in corners, on the floor and on the walls of rooms. Because of its effectiveness and versatility, it is easily worth its price.

The limit of the effective range is about 3½ feet, covering a circle approximately 4 feet in diameter. Flowering plants must be less than 3 feet away. Since the lamp is relatively cooler than others, the tops of plants can be brought comparatively close.

Wonderlite has provided indoor growing with a new dimension and infinitely greater flexibility. We will not mention it as often as fluorescent tubes in our cultural notes on gift plants because it is not a lamp you will use for propagating. But you will find it useful if you are an indoor gardener and particularly good and necessary if you are growing a big plant for a big present. Also it will maintain the large plants that you are using for stem cuttings.

MOISTURE

We've often asserted that, contrary to popular notion, more plants are killed by having too little water than too much. Hobbyists are the ones who overdo kindness to their plants, but they are a small minority. The vast majority of people only have plants for decoration, and they are the ones who are more often prone to neglect them. The most common kind of neglect is failure to water. And, while plants can do with insufficient light and fertilizing for a long time, most of them must have water at frequent intervals. Many will collapse if they are dry for even a single day. In fact, it is not an uncommon experience to find that certain plants start to sag an hour after the soil is dry and will die if not relieved within a very short time. Thus, watering becomes the most important service you perform in an indoor garden—the most time-consuming and requiring the greatest care. It is for this reason that we recommend succulents so strongly to busy or lazy gardeners. It is one category of plants that actually benefits for most of the year from neglect.

The majority of plants prefer being evenly moist at all times. This is impossible, because when we water them, the soil is temporarily clogged. However, if the soil is sufficiently porous and there is no standing water in the tray or saucer, this condition usually lasts for only a short time. That short time does vary, being shorter in hot weather than cool. And it also partly depends on whether the plant is growing actively and immediately starts to absorb some of the moisture, contributing to the drying out process. If the period of clogging is extended, it can cause disease and kill the plant. We must draw the conclusion, then, that with many plants, a thorough watering when the plant is not active and the weather or house is relatively cool is dangerous. On the other hand, as we've pointed out, complete dryness can also be lethal. We have to use good judgement.

The amount of watering varies according to the size of the pot and the behavior of the plant. A small plant in a large pot needs far less water than when there is little soil for its roots. One reason why we pot succulents quite small is not, as so many believe, because the plant likes a tight fit, but because a larger pot with more soil means that at any watering, the soil takes longer to dry out—and wet soil for any long period is something succulents can't stand.

However, once the initial moisture has been reduced so that the soil particles are moist but the spaces between are open and aerated, there is a more-or-less extended period of complete comfort for the plant. It ends when the soil is dry again. Keeping the clogging period as short as possible and the well-aerated, moist condition as long as possible is the secret for growing healthy plants.

Another factor you have to watch is the plant's drinking habits. It won't take you long to discover that different kinds of plants of the same size, in equal pots, have a vastly different degree of thirst. You cannot tell by their appearance which drink more and which less. A juicy plant may use little water and one that has a dry look all the time may drink like a fish. Once you know the drink rate of your plants, you will have a better idea of which ones can be neglected and which can be expected to push the panic button at frequent intervals. If you have any doubts on this subject, just watch the different rates of water consumption of a *Dieffenbachia* and a Lantana. The latter is insatiable.

It does not matter whether you water from the top or bottom of the pot. But when watering from the top, be careful not to wet the plant itself. When water gets in the joints of some plants it starts a rotting process. When watering from the bottom, be careful to remove excess water from the saucer once the soil of the pot is wet.

Various methods are used for providing the soil in pots with a steady flow of controlled moisture. One of these is by means of wicks, which may operate through the top of the soil or through the bottom of the pot. There are also pots made with reservoirs that act in the same way. The advantage is that the soil absorbs water only as it dries and the drenching associated with regular watering is avoided. Many plants do benefit from this treatment. Nevertheless, it is not a universal panacea and there are any number of plants that react badly because they want their soils to dry out nearly completely before being watered again. However, anyone who has to let plants take care of themselves for several days at a time will find wicking or reservoir pots a lifesaver.

Telling how moist or dry soil really is, once the top surface is no longer moist, is not always easy, especially with succulents. We believe that the moisture meter is the modern solution to this problem and one of the best accessories to have for indoor gardening. The type we use has a long metal probe and a dial that shows instantly the amount of moisture. With it, we can tell whether the bottom of the soil is drier than the top. It only takes an instant and is invaluable. We do not recommend any of the plastic moisture indicators for individual pots. They're cheap, but wear out fast and do not go deep enough into the pot.

Here are some simple rules to follow:

1. Always use room temperature water. We draw lukewarm water from the hot water faucet. This also has the advantage that in the pre-heating process, volatile chemicals are evaporated.

2. Reduce watering on plants that are not growing.

3. If a plant in moist soil looks limp, do not water. Check for rot in infected roots or base of stem. Provided these are okay, repot in new, slightly moist soil and place in shade temporarily. If the temperature is above 85 degrees F., move to a cooler place. If the plant is infected, try to root stem cuttings of the still healthy parts.

4. When the temperature is below 65 degrees F. indoors, do not water a plant thoroughly at any time. That means giving less water than is necessary to soak all the soil in the pot.

FERTILIZER

The indoor gardener uses two types of fertilizer, available in small convenient packages or bottles. Most of it is in crystal, granular or powder form and is an inorganic chemical mixture. Fish fertilizer is a liquid organic concentrate, but its fertilizing action is also due to the chemical content.

All fertilizer packages bear a label listing the content of primary plant foods. These are nitrates, phosphates and potash. The percentages are always given in that order. A fertilizer with the label 5-10-5 contains 5 percent nitrates, 10 percent phosphates and 5 percent potash. Fish emulsion is usually 5-1-1, meaning 5 percent nitrates, 1 percent phosphates and 1 percent potash.

A universally applicable formula for most foliage plants is a balanced one such as 20-20-20. Flowering plants should be given a formula with a high phosphate number. Plants that prefer acid conditions—bushes and vines—benefit from a high nitrate number—one at least twice as large as the other two. Acid plants also often require a dose of iron in a form sold as Iron Chelate or Chelated Iron in the shops. Pale leaves are the sign of an iron deficiency.

In addition, there are certain elements especially useful to plants in minute quantities. They are known as trace elements and include boron, copper and magnesium. We prefer packaged fertilizers that also list a content of trace elements.

Unless you keep a record of the amount and frequency with which you fertilize, it is advisable, except with the succulents, to fertilize with every watering. Succulents need fertilizing at rarer intervals—usually with a balanced formula. All the fertilizers dissolve in water. The labels on the packages indicate the amount required to a gallon of water, usually in teaspoons or fractions of teaspoons. When fertilizing with each watering, reduce the amount used to *one fourth* the recommendation on the package.

When the leaf edges of foliage plants yellow, and neither low humidity nor pests can be identified as the cause, try a high potash fertilizer.

Plants do not use all the fertilizer supplied to them. The remainder stays in the soil and gradually builds up a high concentration with each treatment. Accumulated salts in the soil is one of the main reasons why large plants in large pots that have been performing satisfactorily for a long while suddenly give up the ghost. You can prevent this damage by leaching out the salts twice a year. Take the pot to the tub, shower or sink and allow water to soak through the soil for several minutes.

TEMPERATURE

The average American home maintains a minimum temperature of 65 degrees F. in winter. With energy shortages, this could drop to 55 degrees F. The upper level is ideal for most of our tropical plants and for blooming in winter. The lower figure will stop bloom in most plants. The effect on tropical foliage plants varies. Most will just stop growing for a while but will do all right if watered very little. The English, who have always had cool homes in winter, can carry many tropical plants through the cold months by this simple device.

There are homes where low temperatures are preferred in winter, even below 55 degrees F. Such environments are unfriendly to most tropical plants, and this means that the repertory becomes nearly as restricted as in former times. We wish we could suggest temporary gift plants for such homes. But, though the temperature level may be ideal, the lack of humidity and sun makes the culture of most of them impractical.

Air conditioning has the effect of decreasing the humidity. Nevertheless, we have found that the even temperatures and the coolness in summer are very beneficial. In most of the country, we would rather grow tropical plants with air conditioning than without it. High-humidity plants can be concentrated in one area of a room—for instance in shelving—and a humidifier placed directly in front of it. If the humidifier is unsightly, you can plan to put it away in a closet when visitors are expected.

Even experienced amateurs are usually unaware of the severe damage to be expected from a period of excessively high temperatures. Nor are they familiar with the fact that tropical temperatures never reach the 100-degree and higher mark that is often achieved in the dog days of July and August in the interior of the country.

Above 85 degrees F., plant metabolism speeds up, and at 90 degrees F. or higher, heat prostration can set in. Northern humidity levels are also lower than tropical ones and this also contributes to the discomfort of the plant. Keep a watch on this phenomenon during very hot days. At the first sign of suffering, get the plants out from sun or from under artificial light and place them in a relatively cool situation in the shade. Don't water unless the soil is bone dry, and then do so only sparingly each day until the plant recovers.

Also in summer, watch out for your terrariums. If the inner temperature goes way up, gray mold can engulf all the plants in a single night. Open up the top, partially or all the way, to prevent this from happening.

Also, keep a sharp lookout for the condition of stem cuttings, leaf cuttings and seedlings, especially those in covered propagating boxes. They, too, may need airing and a temporary removal from light. Mist with an antidamp-off fungicide.

HUMIDITY

Tropical and greenhouse nurseries operate at a humidity level over 65 percent at all times. Complemented by high average temperatures, this causes speedy growth. Summer indoor levels in most of the country reflect high outdoor humidity. In winter, the indoor level drops very low, aggravated by central heating. Air conditioning has a *de-humidifying* effect summer and winter. Since indoor growers do not desire rapid foliage plant growth, a 50 percent level is satisfactory for the majority of tropical foliage plants and a good many of these can thrive on considerably less throughout the year. On the other hand, almost all the flowering plants need at least 50 percent humidity to induce blooming.

To raise humidity around plants, modern indoor growers often use trays that they fit with plastic crate and then partly fill with water. Plastic crate is a diffuser sheet often seen in the ceilings of elevators. Usually ½-inch thick, it has square or hexagonal openings. Pots are set on its surface. This has many advantages over wet pebbles—the light weight and the ease of cleaning are two of these. The crate can be bought from plastic suppliers in 2x4-foot sheets. Often, scrap sizes can be bought and are more economical.

This method helps, but is never entirely satisfactory. Far better is a room humidifier. There are small, 1-gallon capacity models that are quite efficient but must be refilled daily when in use. In the long run, you are much better off with an 8- to 12-gallon reservoir model that should also be provided with a hygrometer that measures humidity and will turn the machine on only when the level falls below the percentage you have set on the dial. These machines last for years and pay for themselves.

In any event, it is advisable to have a hygrometer hung somewhere near your indoor garden. Otherwise, you will never know why some of your best plants do poorly in winter. Aware that the humidity is far below what the plants require, you can take measures to improve the environment.

POTS and POTTING

Of the two kinds of utility pots, clay and plastic, we prefer plastic. We agree that, initially, clay is better looking, and we regret that it has so many disadvantages for indoor gardening. The worst is its porous quality, which causes soil to dry out rapidly. This does not happen in a greenhouse because of the humidity and the way the pots are packed close to each other. But in the house it is very noticeable. Clay pots also take up more room with their thick walls and thicker rims. Space is at a premium indoors. The clay, it should also be mentioned, is a happier hunting ground for insects than is plastic. Finally, the material does not retain its clean appearance for long. When a plant has been in clay for six months or more, fertilizer and soil salts penetrate the wall and ooze through to the outside. All the effort in the world will thereafter be inadequate to restore the pot to its original appearance.

We often *do* use clay pots for succulents and other plants that require quick drying out. In these cases, the porosity of the clay is an advantage.

Whereas clay pots only come in rounds, plastic ones can be bought in rounds and squares. The square pots fit together neatly and, especially where small plants are concerned (which happens when you are propagating actively), can be packed into much smaller spaces and in a more orderly manner. At a slight increase in cost, very good colors can be bought in plastic—a rust-red and a deep green that are most attractive.

When choosing a pot for a transplant or a re-potting, pick the smallest workable size—one that will just accommodate the roots and soil comfortably. In that way, you are much less likely to over-water even if you are careless on this point. That means more re-potting in a shorter time. But if you are engaged in plant gifting, that will not be a drawback.

There are two solutions available to you when you are ready to make a present and desire a better-looking container. One is to transplant to an art pot, allowing somewhat more room for the roots so that the recipient doesn't have to repot too quickly. The other is to use a cache-pot. This is simply an art pot that acts as a container for an ordinary pot. The advantage of the second method is that it involves no immediate transplanting and offers the recipient the means to use the cache-pot as the growing pot later on when the plant is bigger. Cache-pots can also be switched at will, leaving the choice up to the recipient. Some decorative containers of glazed ceramic make poor growing pots, and the plant is then far better off in its original container with the cache-pot as an outside cover.

Indoor gardeners no longer put drainage materials in the bottoms of their pots. That is a custom normal in nursery or greenhouse practice as a means of preventing excessive moisture. It is not a problem in the house and only wastes space. Porous soilless mixes provide sufficient soil aeration without the use of pebbles or pieces of clay pots in the bottom.

Fine foliage shrub, *Pittosporum tobira*, in a superb art pot for a housewarming, shower or birthday present.

Except with pots we use in terrariums, we do not cover the bottom holes. We like to know when our plants are truly pot bound, and that is only possible if we can look into the bottom of the pot or if some piece of root grows out through one of the holes. In a terrarium, where the pot is imbedded in soilless mix, we do not want those roots to take off through the holes; hence, we have to plug the bottom. For this purpose, a piece of plastic window screening is all that is needed.

Repotting is a simple matter. Contrary to some experts, we always moisten the soil of the plant to be repotted, but we do not carry through the entire process immediately. When the soil is just moist, it will stick together when removed from the pot. It will not do that if it is either bone dry or soaking wet.

When the soil has become free of excess moisture—usually after a few hours—we up-end the pot and rap the edge on a hard object, whereupon the whole of the root and the soil ball comes free without any disturbance. The rest is only a matter of fitting it into the new pot. First, you have to put some soil in the bottom if the pot is taller so that the plant will have its base below the rim of the new pot—but only a little. Secondly, you have to fill in the open spaces with fresh soil.

There is one problem with plastic pots which requires attention when potting or repotting. That is, plastic pots are so shaped that there is a shelf below the rim. If you fill the pot with soil above this shelf, it is easy to leave an invisible airspace all around the sides.

This is a frequent cause of trouble because, when such a pot is watered, the liquid runs down the sides and fails to penetrate the soil. We have known instances when a plant has failed after being watered twice a day. If the plant and its pot were brought to us, we soon discovered the trouble that completely puzzled the owner who, more often than not, had the impression that the plant was failing because of excess moisture.

To prevent this situation and any other open spaces in the soil around the roots, use a potting stick. It is no more than a dowel or other round piece of wood which has been given a blunt, two-edged point. For small pots, a small dowel will do. For large ones, a length of discarded broomstick is ideal.

With this tool, tamp down the soil along the edges and in the corners of the pot. It may also be necessary to drive the stick down into the pot along the inner wall and lever the soil inward, making room for additional material and filling in any interior spaces. By doing this, which applies pressure from the outside inward, you avoid damage to the roots. Never drive down the soil in the center of the pot.

With time, many plants develop a large root system without a corresponding increase in the size of the plant above soil level. When this happens, transplanting to a larger pot is unsatisfactory as the plant will appear to be proportionately too small. Decant the plant and cut off at least half of the roots so that the plant can be put back in the old pot with new soil.

A close relative of the Ming Aralia, *Polyscias balfouriana* is an easy and showy foliage plant.

PESTS

There are so many articles and books, including our own, that treat the matter of insect pests at some length, we will restrict this section to stating our preferences for combatting infestations.

The principal pests of house plants are the following:

Mealybugs are white, powdery, slow-moving creatures that often surround themselves with a mass of transparent goo. They are visible and unmistakeable.

Scale insects are colorless to dark brown, shiny, oval scales.

Mites are tiny spiders invisible to the naked eye.

White fly are beautiful, small-winged creatures like tiny white moths.

They multiply at a tremendous rate and do considerable damage.

There are a number of small soil insects, black and white, that do little if any harm and are merely an annoyance.

In order to discover mites, which are the most destructive of these pests, you would be well advised to equip yourself with a 10 power magnifying glass or loupe, sold through hobby shops, household repair catalogs and gadget distributors. Since almost every indoor garden sooner or later suffers an invasion of mites, you should check your plants whenever there is any leaf drop or signs of leaf damage without any visible cause.

In our treatment of pest infestations, we have tried to eliminate pesticides entirely. They are nasty to handle and potentially dangerous to health. Some of the most effective ones are being banned for use by amateurs, and with good reason. Labels of pesticide packages usually list a number of precautions permitting use with safety. These involve the use of masks, gloves and special clothing. In our experience, amateurs do not follow these instructions in detail and therefore expose themselves to very active poisonous substances. Admittedly, doing all the things required is a major nuisance and, if the instructions were taken seriously, most people would rather abandon the plants. We think it is better to look for other ways of getting rid of the pests.

Mealybugs and scale insects can be removed from plants, and killed in the process, by using a broad soft brush dipped in rubbing alcohol. Work over the under surfaces of the leaves and in the joints of the leaf stalks. Even if you see no more of the pests, repeat the process at least three times at intervals of three days. Meanwhile, keep a sharp watch on any plants nearby in order to observe any sign that they are also infected.

If your fern plant has scales, cut off all the leaves and drench the plant in a solution of 1 tablespoon of bleach to a quart of water. Davallias are most frequently attacked. Coarser ferns can be treated with the rubbing alcohol method.

If you discover mites on your plants, take them to the kitchen sink or anywhere they can be subjected to the strongest jet of water. Turn the plant upside down, holding plant and soil with one hand and, if necessary, with a piece of plastic over the soil, and direct the water at the undersides of the leaves. Do not fear damage from the force of the jet. Only sick leaves will come off. Use water that is lukewarm or at least room temperature. Repeat the process every three days over a period of nine days.

If this does not work, try spraying the undersides of the leaves with House and Garden Raid. Hold the plant quite close to the can so that the surface is creamed by the pesticide. Some plants may suffer damage, but the majority will not, and results are usually satisfactory.

We also use the washing or Raid method with white fly. Because the fly produces a new generation every two days, there are new ones being hatched every day. But continuous washings and two or three treatments with Raid usually works. When you have discovered white fly, separate the affected plants from the others until you are sure that the infestation is done for.

Small soil insects can be killed off by using a drench of Nicotine sulphate, Black Leaf 40. Even a solution of detergent often does the trick. But be careful to wipe all exposed surfaces of the pot at the same time. These little creatures are relatively fast moving and dodge around on the surfaces.

We leave nematodes to the last. These are minute worms attacking roots or leaves. You can see them on leaves with a 10 power loupe, doing tightrope walking along the edge. They are not so easy to see in the soil, but evidence of their presence are small nodules that don't belong on the fine roots. Nematodes are so dangerous to all your plants that our first line of advice is to throw out the plant. However, if it is very dear to you, there is no other solution than to use Kelthane, a stinky liquid pesticide which kills them off. Spray the plant or drench the soil as the case may be and take *every precaution* in handling this material that the label recommends.

DISEASES

Most diseases of indoor and other plants are from fungi or virus. There is no cure for a virused plant. It is almost impossible for an amateur to diagnose the disease. The plant will die and there is no way of saving it. As for fungi, by the time they have killed off roots or the base of stems, their favorite areas, there is nothing you can do except save any healthy parts and use them as cuttings for propagation. A few fungal problems, such as gray mold and damp-off, can be treated with a number of sprays on the market.

Terrariums as Gifts

Terrariums are so important in gift giving that they deserve a special discussion of culture. Recently they have been less popular, not because of any shortcomings of terrariums, but due to the flooding of the commercial market with improperly planted containers. So many of these terrariums did not function that there was a good deal of disillusion, aggravated by the fact that most were by no means inexpensive. But terrariums have so many advantages that you must always keep them in mind whenever giving is involved.

Not everybody understands what a terrarium really is. It is not an open glass container. Quite the contrary, it is any clear container with a transparent cover. For instance, the plastic shoe box we use for propagating could be used as a terrarium, although we don't do so because, unless used for scientific investigation, we expect containers to be not only efficient but also good-looking. That is why we prefer fish tanks, plastic and glass bowls with covers, and the handsome leaded- or brass-bound models that you can purchase in stores or, if you're handy, can make yourself.

TERRARIUM SHAPES and MATERIALS

We have mentioned standard globe and fish tank terrariums. Both are available in many sizes. In addition, there are beautiful leaded glass models on the market and some very attractive ones with brass fittings.

Glass is preferable to plastic because the latter invariably scratches or discolors with time. Don't believe anyone who tells you that they have a plastic that remains crystal clear. Only glass is permanent and can be reused. A large number of firms make all kinds of interesting shapes besides those mentioned above.

Bottles, including the commercial-use carboys, can be adapted to terrarium plantings or "bottle gardens", or you can buy special jugs that are manufactured as decorative bottle garden containers. The use of these containers is exactly the same as any other terrarium. The only difference is the narrow opening. Since the leaves of plants fold upward without breaking, they can be stuffed through the opening. By means of long instruments—there are kits on the market—you can move the plants around, dig holes, and firm the soil. Little bottles with tiny plants are fine for the benefit sale table and for small gifting. A large, carefully planted carboy can be as impressive a gift as any other terrarium.

ADVANTAGES of TERRARIUM GROWING

Because terrariums are closed containers, the environment inside is stable and the top has to be removed only on rare occasions. It is possible to keep plants in hermetically sealed vessels for years. No ventilation is necessary, no fertilizer, no additional watering. Light is provided from the outside. So the only influence that can disturb a terrarium is temperature. It will cease to function if too cold and succumb to fungal diseases if too hot, which can happen on hot summer days if the top is not opened to relieve the heat inside.

Carefully planted containers that are grown for their beauty need to be groomed—dead leaves removed, plants trimmed, or over-grown plants removed and replaced with smaller plants. But, if the plants are

A fibrous rooted angel wing Begonia flourishes here. The top of the terrarium is left off for the photograph. A delightful present for the ill.

chosen with care and are started when small, a terrarium can usually go without attention for at least a year. That means that it is possible to present it to a person who either does not know how to or cannot give it proper care. Sick people, beginners and very busy people are ideal recipients of terrariums.

Secondly, we cannot ignore the fact that the container and careful planting makes a more beautiful gift than almost any other form that plant gifting can take. Both plantings and containers can be as simple or as complex, as inexpensive or as costly as you wish.

An advantage that people are always forgetting is that terrariums are a protection for your plants against cats and, usually, inquisitive children. They are also sealed against insect pests. If they become infested, you can be sure the pests were there when the terrarium was closed.

While it's preferable that the terrarium container be beautiful as well as utilitarian, a very plain one *will* serve the purpose. Glass jam or peanut butter jars, glass cannisters, and a myriad of other simple household containers become terrariums the moment they have tight-fitting plastic covers. One plastic old-fashioned glass can serve as the bottom of a terrarium and the other as the top. If you have two slightly different sized glasses, either one can be top or bottom.

Young plants are often best started in this environment, and it is therefore the best way of giving such a plant to someone who cannot take care of it properly in the early stages—for instance, a house guest who would like a small plant to take with them, a frequent occurrence. The utilitarian terrarium protects the potted plant for several weeks against the rigors

Landscaped terrarium with two-tube fluorescent fixture. A fine gift for anniversary or retirement.

of an environmental change. But you must warn your guest to "harden off" the plant by opening the top gradually over a period of a week or two before letting it join other plants on a shelf or window sill.

It should also be pointed out that when the home environment is unsuitable for a tropical plant because of unreliable heat or insufficient humidity, a terrarium is the surest way of growing temporarily or permanently. It is almost a guarantee of a blooming environment for the smaller tropical plants that need high humidity.

Thus, the terrarium is not only a decorative furnishing for the home but also one of the most useful means of growing exotic plants indoors without the need to make drastic changes in the environment.

PREPARING the SOIL

There is only one difficulty in preparing a terrarium. You must remember that this environment is closed and that the moisture inside must be exactly balanced to supply the growing needs and the aerial humidity. This moisture is constantly recirculating, as is the air within the container. Any excess moisture creates a sauna atmosphere that will quickly kill any plant. Any free water is there to stay and will rot out the roots. But once you have balanced the moisture, the terrarium functions automatically and needs no further attention.

The moisture factor is so critical that we advise preparing the soil well ahead of time on the first few tries so that you can learn just how much water to add with the brand of components you are using.

The soil of our terrariums is a 1-1-1 soilless mix, or in other words, 1 part sphagnum peat moss, 1 part vermiculite and 1 part perlite. If you are going to use tropical exotics or any other plants besides northern woodland wild plants in the terrarium, you should add 4 tablespoons of lime chips or crushed eggshell to the quart of mix. This is equivalent to 2 tablespoons of powdered lime.

Stir up the mix in a bowl and add ¾ cup of water to a quart of the mix. Stir well, cover and leave overnight. The next day, test the feel of the mix. If it is wet, there is too much water. If it does not feel slightly moist all through, it is too dry. The particles of the mix must be light and separated and just perceptibly moist. If you have too much water, add ½ pint of soil; if too dry, add ¼ cup water to the mix. Test overnight again to be sure it is just right. This test is necessary because some brands of peat moss, perlite or vermiculite do not absorb water in the same way as other brands. But once you have the right formula, you can use it repeatedly, and the rest of your terrarium gardening will be easy.

Provided the balance is right, you are now ready for planting.

CHOOSING PLANTS

As we mentioned, it is important to choose the plants for your terrarium with care. The following is a partial list of plants suitable for landscaped terrariums. All of them thrive in a temperature range of 65 to 85 degrees F.

Begonias. Any of the many species and hybrids with small leaves.

Calathea insignis, micans, picturata, stromata, trifasciata and *van den heckei.*

Dichorisandra reginae.

Ferns. Maidenhair types (Asplenium) and *Polystichum tsus-simense.*

Ficus pumila.

Fittonia. Small-leaved kinds.

Geogenanthus undatus.

Gesneria cuneifolia. An everblooming relative of the African Violet.

Helxine soleiroli. Baby's Tears.

Koellikeria erinoides.

Marantas. Prayer Plants.

Pellionia daveauana and *pulchra.*

Peperomia petiolata, caprata, obtusifolia and 'Astrid'.

Pilea cadierei, depressa, involucrata and *microphylla.*

Polyscias fruticosa.

Rosmarinus prostratus. Rosemary.

Saintpaulia. African Violets.

Sansevieria 'Hahnii'.

Selaginella. All species.

Serissa foetida marginata.

Sinningia. Miniatures such as 'Bright Eyes', 'Cindy' or 'Cindy-Ella', 'Doll Baby', 'Freckles'.

CULTURE

When you use a small container to hold a single small plant, the depth of soil it will accommodate is shallow and planting directly into the soil is unavoidable. This usually causes no problems because you expect the roots of that one plant to spread through the soil and if it does not do well it can be replaced without trouble.

The situation is very different in a large terrarium with several plants. Roots are not confined to one spot but intermingle, so that when you have to move or remove a plant, it can be done only at the cost of ripping the design apart and disturbing the roots of other plants. Replacing plants then becomes a complicated task.

For these reasons, all plants for our larger terrariums are in plastic pots with a piece of screening in the bottom to prevent the roots from growing through into the medium. The depth of soil is usually sufficient to cover the pots, and, in a pinch, stones set in the soil can hide their rims. This allows plants to be removed and replaced very easily and, if individual watering or fertilizing is required, we can confine our efforts to one plant without disturbing others.

We should add that, once you have planted your terrarium and covered it, should you have made any mistake in the moisture content, it will become evident within a few days. The side of the terrarium away from heat or the source of light will cloud up normally. Even if it does not do this, you are still probably well-balanced. Expect trouble only if the top or sides collect water drops that run down. Then you *do* have too much moisture. To correct, remove the cover until the excess moisture has evaporated. Test after each 12-hour period by placing the cover over the top for 12 hours. If moisture still collects and runs down the sides, take off the cover for another 12 hours.

After a terrarium is closed, it rarely needs attention to keep the plants alive. But when you are dealing with modern, carefully designed plantings, two problems can arise.

One is that to maintain appearances, some adjustments of position and some grooming may be necessary. This is far easier done when plants are in individual plastic pots, but it does involve opening the top of the terrarium and releasing internal moisture.

The other problem is that, whether terrariums are placed under fluorescent fixtures or in the Bright Reflected light from a window, without air conditioning there occur periods in summer when the heat is excessive. At such times, it is necessary to open the cover in part or all the way. Evaporation takes place and the moisture must be replaced. Do so carefully in proportion to the amount of soil in the container so that balance is properly restored. At that time, some fertilizer can be applied.

LANDSCAPING a TERRARIUM

A little terrarium with a single miniature plant needs no other decorations than, say, a surface of bird gravel with, possibly, a miniature novelty ornament at its base.

Large terrariums that are carefully landscaped are among the most appreciated of all gifts for important occasions. As a birthday, anniversary, wedding or retirement gift, a landscaped terrarium is virtually sure to please, and its look of permanence is the same as a picture or a piece of fine furniture. Such terrariums are like shadow boxes containing a miniature world and they enhance any setting.

In general, we use beautiful stones as our main contrast to soil and plants. On one side, the soil is built up high; at another, only pebbles cover the base. In this way, the landscape can be terraced and offers more variety. (See the photo/caption sequence below for some basic steps. We also refer readers to our book, *Fun With Terrarium Gardening*, for the step-by-step design and building of these landscapes.)

It is a mistake with such terrariums to crowd the plants. Carefully place just a few young, under-sized plants that still have a way to grow before the landscape reaches its peak. If you plant perfectly at the start, the appearance of the scene will start to deteriorate. Instead, leave plenty of room between plants and make the view interesting with stones and other accessories, until you have created a miniature world.

SOME BASIC STEPS IN BUILDING A LANDSCAPED TERRARIUM

1. Large and small stones are used to build landscapes. Black or white Japanese pebbles are a decorative covering for the lowest level in the arrangement. The only other materials are soilless mix and perlite (see text).

2. A 10-gallon tropical fish tank. There are many sizes to choose from. Lay down a half-inch base of perlite. Over that build up your low and high hills. The highest points should always be against the glass.

3. Digging a hole for a pot.

4. The partly finished arrangement. Pots are hidden by soil and stones. Other stones act as supports for the soil or as decorative accents.

5. Other plants have been added and the lowest level covered with Japanese pebbles. A gentle stream of water directed against the glass panes will clean the inner surfaces.

TERRARIUMS with FREE-STANDING POTS

Set one or more pots of plants in a terrarium without embedding them in soil. One rarely sees such arrangements, although they are the simplest to put together and make some of the most sumptuous of gifts.

A square or rectangular terrarium may be the most satisfactory. Pave the bottom of the terrarium in a decorative way with pebbles or any attractive material. Then prepare two or more small plants in decorative containers and arrange them in the terrarium. Water the pots well and close the top with a fitted piece of glass. To make an attractive setting, add a sheet of mirror on the back of the terrarium. Then use small colorful rocks, art objects such as Japanese miniatures, or pieces of driftwood as decorative accents to enrich the design.

One of the great advantages of this gift is that the plants will need no attention for a long time and that, if anything does happen to them, they are easily replaced. Even difficult plants can be enjoyed by a beginner.

Culinary herbs in a terrarium. They need less care this way. Later, the pots can be removed and the container used for a regular planting. A big gift for a special occasion, but modest in cost. Cover is left off for photograph.

Propagating Plants for Gift Giving

Multiplying plants is so much a part of the pleasures and rewards of indoor growing that we cannot conceive of doing without it. Watching seeds come up and develop into the plants we love is always fascinating. Seeing a sprig or woody section of a plant growing roots below and new greenery above is equally enjoyable. Best of all, propagation is as useful as it is pleasurable.

Whenever we buy a new plant, we immediately take a cutting if possible, and root it. That way, even if our acquisition fails to survive the shock of a changed environment, the cutting usually lives, and all is not lost. This insurance is particularly welcome if the plant is hard to come by. We also face the fact that many plants have a rather short life span. Rather than exposing ourselves to the necessity of shopping for new ones, we always have rooted cuttings as a backup.

Extensive plant gift giving is almost unthinkable without some facility in propagating. That is how you grow sufficient quantities of the desirable plants. We grow plants from seeds when we need a large number of plants all at one time. We seed many annuals and a number of plants that are difficult to root from cuttings. But wherever cuttings are possible and convenient, they have priority.

In this chapter, we describe our methods of multiplying plants and the soil formulas we use with the plants in our cultural plant list. Theory is of little assistance in such matters. In order to be prepared to grow many plants for gift giving throughout the year, you have to practice what we preach. At first you may have a few failures, but you will soon learn from your mistakes. And from then on, propagation will become as nearly automatic as growing plants can be.

STEM CUTTINGS

Advantages of Stem Propagation. For indoor gardeners, the most convenient and satisfactory way of multiplying plants is by means of stem cuttings. We have found that it is the best way of handling the majority of tropical plants. It is the method we always try first unless it is obvious that it will not work. There are two major advantages. One is that new plants will be exactly like the parent. You do not have to worry, as you do with seeds, that they will have leaves and flowers of a different color or shape—or even a different way of growing—than expected. The other advantage is that the moment the cutting is rooted, you have a small but nearly mature plant. With seed, you are starting from scratch, so the plant usually takes a much longer time to reach maturity.

Types of plants. Well-branched plants supply the largest number of cuttings. If you make a practice of pruning them when young, they will not only become more shapely and compact, but will also develop a greater number of branches. When the plant is more mature, normal pruning continues. The trimmings can often be rooted; you should not throw them away without considering this possibility.

There are a few single-stemmed plants which can be cut into a number of lengths and rooted, virtually destroying the parent in the process. Dieffenbachias are often handled in this way when they grow too tall and unsightly. But don't attempt this with palm trees or with some single-stemmed succulent euphorbias which will not root at all if cut into pieces. In these instances, you must seek other means of accomplishing the job.

Woody-shrubby plants are another category. The harder the wood, the greater the difficulty in producing roots. Azaleas, the branches of young trees, etc., often either take a very long time to root, or fail to absorb and use moisture, ending up by drying out completely. But a thick stem is not necessarily a bad cutting. Thick, juicy stems and branches of some tropical plants—Allamanda, Frangipani and Drymonia are good examples—root easily if treated properly.

Every plant has its own way of responding to different methods of propagating. There is no uniform rule. Don't take for granted that plants with the same genus name can be propagated in the same way. Some Oxalis, for instance, have fibrous roots and normal branches. But others have no stems and their pips must be propagated by separating them (see Division, pg. 74). Some cacti root easily from sections of stem, while others produce offsets. If neither method is suitable, you may have to grow all new plants from seed.

Taking the cutting. Most experts disapprove of scissors for taking a cutting because a dull pair will squeeze the stem, causing damage. But scissors are very handy and, as long as they are clean and *very* sharp, they will do the job on the usual thin stems or branches. Little horticultural scissors are often included in indoor gardening tool kits.

If the stem is thick and woody, no scissors can deal with it—a special knife is required. It is called a pruning knife or secateur, and usually has a short, broad, curved blade. This is the same kind of knife that is used to prune fruit trees.

Where to cut—the joints. Every stem and branch of a plant is divided into joints or nodes where branches, twigs or leaves are attached. The stem or branch is always thickened at that point. The joints may encircle the whole stem or branch, or consist of swellings with a leaf or smaller branch-scar arranged opposite each other, alternately, or opposite *and* alternately. The arrangement really makes very little difference in taking cuttings, as long as you recognize the swellings as joints.

Make the slice just below a joint. The first cutting from a branch is made two or three or more joints from the tip. That one can be made straight across the stem or at an angle. But if you take more cuttings further down the stem, it is important to indicate which end is up. Planting a cutting on its head is poor policy and unfortunately it is possible to make a whole set of mid-branch cuttings and then totally forget in which direction they originally grew on the plant. The only way to prevent any mistake of this kind is to cut each section to a point, or wedge, at the bottom end. The wedge end is always the one to be planted in the soil.

Size of the cutting. The length of a cutting depends on the distance between the joints. Very often a cutting consisting of two joints is satisfactory while three joints are usually better. The point is that one joint must always be covered by soil when the cutting is planted, and one must be above ground. If the joints are far enough apart, two or three joints are ample. But if the plant happens to have them very close together so that there are, say, a half dozen to an inch, you may end up needing 12 joints, of which four or more will be buried.

Then there is the question of how big a plant you want as a starter. Often that does not matter and you will take the length of cutting which is practical and at the same time does the least damage to the parent plant. But if you are planning to have several small pots of foliage or flowering plants as gifts, you should take a cutting which is sufficiently large to be suitable as a gift as soon as it is rooted.

Removing flowers and excess leaves. The objective in propagating from cuttings is to induce the piece of stem to produce roots. When a section of branch set in moist soil has a full complement of leaves, these leaves will continue to function. The cutting may even put out new side shoots and leaves. Using its energy in this way deprives the cutting of its ability to produce roots. Eventually, the leaves stop growing and the cutting starves to death. Attempting to propagate from a cutting that has buds and flowers is even more difficult because, with plants, as with every other living thing, the most direct means of reproduction takes priority. Therefore, buds and flowers absorb all the energy of the cutting.

That is the reason why you should remove all flowers and buds and any large clusters of leaves, leaving only a few which are necessary to provide energy, but not so many as to monopolize it. When the cutting is taken from the tip of a branch, always nip off the leading growth of leaves, thereby discouraging new growth. In addition, the section of the cutting which is to be buried in the soil must be bare of branches and leaves. Always cut these off close to the main stem.

Rooting cuttings is easy. Rooting cuttings is a simple matter requiring no great skill or attention. Nevertheless, you will not be equally successful ever time. Don't be discouraged. Sometimes every single one of a large number of cuttings roots for us. In another batch, some will not, for reasons we cannot always fathom. Home conditions do change and are not always equally favorable to the plants. No matter how specific the directions we give, everyone varies the method slightly. By observing the reactions of your plants during your first attempts, you can learn how to adjust and achieve better results.

Growing mediums for stem cuttings. All growing mediums for stem cuttings must be sterilized and should contain little or no plant nourishment. Packaged soils sold by plant shops, florists and garden centers are

From the left, vermiculite, peat moss and perlite in the tray. In the prop box is the mixture, and after seeding, a thin coating of milled sphagnum moss has been spread on the surface to the right.

pre-sterilized. However, any material you dig up out-of-doors should be sterilized by baking in an oven at 180 degrees F. for a half hour.

The three most commonly used soil components are vermiculite, perlite and gritty sand. Each of these can be used alone. Sometimes half and half vermiculite and perlite is a good combination. Garden soil must be mixed with one-third perlite or one-third vermiculite or a combination of both. No one of these soils is necessarily better than the others and each person, depending on the growing environment, may prefer one to the other. We have always favored vermiculite except for the cuttings that root most easily. These benefit from soilless mixes because they need not be transferred from one soil to another and continue to grow in the same mix in which they have been rooted.

Prop boxes. Prop box—short for propagation box—is the indoor gardening slang abbreviation used to indicate any container for multiplying plants. We'll use this term throughout, because there is no other special name for the various kinds of open and closed containers used in propagating. Depth of the prop box is important—*there must be at least two inches of soil.* Closed containers should have enough room for an inch of growth over the height of the cutting that is used. Plants from dry climates usually prefer the open container method of propagation and those from very warm, tropical, humid climates respond to the closed container method. Some cuttings will die off in an open container. Others, if placed in a closed, humid atmosphere, immediately succumb to fungal diseases. We suggest trying the closed prop box method first. If this does not work, try your next cuttings in an open box.

Open prop boxes. An open prop box may be made of plastic, baked clay or wood. It can be the bottom of a waxed or plastic milk carton or a round freezer container. It need not be of transparent material. And, since it can also be an ordinary flower pot, "box" is something of a misnomer. Make holes in the bottom.

As for size, that is a matter of how many cuttings of a certain length or thickness you want to plant. Leave at least a half inch of free space around each cutting. A plastic old-fashioned glass with holes in the bottom is large enough to accommodate four or five small cuttings or a single large one. The bottoms of plastic bread boxes are excellent for a large number of normal house plant cuttings. The cuttings need not all be of the same kind. As long as all are of a type which responds to the open prop box method, you can have as much variety as you wish.

Planting cuttings in open prop boxes. Fill the container to a minimum depth of 2 inches with any one of the recommended soils moistened thoroughly with lukewarm water.

Cuttings of herbs being planted in the prop box.

Dip the lower end of your cutting in a hormone powder such as Hormodin or Rootone, and shake off the excess. Whether either of these always aids rooting is questionable, but both do sterilize the open wound of the cutting.

With a pencil or other round stick, poke a hole in the soil and insert the cutting to a depth of an inch or more. Firm the soil around it.

Growing conditions. It is important to realize that a cutting without roots should not be subjected to intense light. Rather, it should have reflected light or a position toward the ends of, and not too close to, fluorescent tubes. We allow a distance of at least 6 inches. The reason for this is that the cutting is much like a sick person, requiring rest, warmth, good air, some light and a tranquil environment in which low energy can be used most effectively.

The temperature should stand at 65 degrees F. or higher at all times, with 75 to 80 degrees F. being ideal. If your home is not warm enough, you may have to place a heating cable under the box. These are sold in sizes suitable for standard indoor gardening trays by mail-order seedsmen, garden centers, etc. If the container is of large size, use the cable under the soil. Where house temperatures are minimum 65 degrees F., fluorescent lighting virtually guarantees proper temperature because the tubes usually raise the level by about 10 degrees. Coolness combined with excess moisture will lead to fungal infections.

The soil should not be constantly wet. After the first moistening, allow the soil surface to dry out. Then spray the surface and the cuttings themselves every day, enough to keep the soil moderately moist.

Given these conditions, cuttings rarely take more than a couple of weeks to start rooting.

Divisions of foil used in a make-shift open prop box with vermiculite. If the cuttings need high humidity, the box can be closed into a clear plastic bag.

Closed prop boxes. The materials and sizes of the container are the same as those of an open container. But the box must have a tight transparent cover and there must be *no* drainage holes.

We use anything that is handy. A single cutting in a small pot we often simply enclose in a clear plastic bag sealed with a Twist-Em or string. You can use one plastic old-fashioned glass as a bottom container and invert another on top of it, creating a small terrarium. We use all types of plastic refrigerator storage boxes with fitted covers. Plastic bread boxes with tight transparent covers have enough space for a large number of cuttings.

The soils are the same as for open prop boxes—vermiculite, perlite or sand—but we rarely use soilless mix or garden soil.

Soil moisture. The amount of moisture in the soil of closed prop boxes is *absolutely* critical. If moisture is excessive in the closed container, the cuttings will quickly rot. Therefore, you must moisten very, very carefully. This is the only difficult part of the whole propagating process, and once you have mastered the trick, success is virtually guaranteed.

It is a matter of adding water to the dry soil very patiently and slowly, very much like adding the proper amount of milk to flour for pancakes. As you know, a point is reached where a very slight amount of additional liquid causes a drastic change in the consistency of the mix.

Pour *lukewarm* water very slowly from a small pitcher or a measuring cup. Stir it in thoroughly, testing the feel of the mix with your fingers. The moment you can sense that there is moisture distributed throughout the mix—in other words, that all the particles have absorbed some water—it is time to stop. The soil must *not* feel wet. Another way of expressing it is that the moisture should be just barely perceptible.

This slight amount of moisture—provided it permeates the soil completely—is all the cuttings need. Once the cuttings have been planted, the container is closed and is never opened—except for root testing—until the cuttings have grown satisfactory roots. The amount of moisture in the tightly closed prop box will not change during this period and therefore need not be replaced. Inside the box, some of the moisture goes into the air and creates the high percentage of humidity which keeps the stems and leaves fresh. The cuttings are forced to reach out into the soil for sustenance. Thus, they are induced to form roots quite rapidly.

Planting and growing. Poke holes in the soil with a round tool, dust the cut and tip of your cutting with hormone powder and insert it in the soil to a depth of at least 1 inch. Cover the container, making sure that it is virtually airtight.

Do not disturb and do not open the container for at least a week. Place it in indirect light—never in sunlight—or toward the ends of the fluorescent tubes.

We repeat: The cuttings require a minimum of 65 degrees F. to root. As it is usually warmer than room temperature under fluorescent lamps, the ideal level of 75 to 80 degrees F. is usually attained in a light garden. However, if you have no warm situation available, you will have to use a heating cable. Where large area containers are being used, the cable can be placed on the bottom and the soil filled in over it. But most people do not realize that containers can also be placed *over* a short cable in trays in a light garden. From one to several prop boxes, depending on size, can be accommodated. The boxes may be slightly tilted by having the wire run under them, but this does no harm.

Testing and hardening the cuttings. After a week has passed, lift the cover of the container and give a cutting a slight tug. It is easy to feel whether there is resistance. If there is none, replace the cover and try again the following week. Test at weekly intervals. Pulling a cutting free

Cuttings are well-rooted and ready for transplanting.

in the very light soil will do it no harm. You can poke it right back in again. Do not remove the plant from the propagation box prematurely. Wait until there is a substantial amount of root, not just one or two spindly ones. Even then, you will have to "harden off" the plant.

When it is evident that the cuttings have enough root, you can accustom them to the idea of living outside the box (hardening off). You do this by opening the container a little more every day. If the container is in a plastic bag, cut holes in the bag in increasing numbers. Should the soil become dryish, which can easily happen now that the cover is partly removed, you can add more water to the soil without serious danger of infection and even use diluted fertilizer at the same time, as you do on your potted plants.

When the cover has finally been removed, your cutting is ready for transplanting to a regular pot filled with soilless potting mix. The pot you choose may even be the one you wish to use as a gift, especially if the cutting is of the right size.

Water propagation of stem cuttings. The only real alternative to rooting cuttings in sterile soil is dangling them in water. We have recourse to this method as a last resort, because the roots grown in water are very delicate and often fail to develop normally when potted up. Water propagation does often succeed with woody plants, especially those which are thick and somewhat soft.

Cut off a piece of branch at least 4 inches long and remove any leaves that will be under water. Set it in a glass of tap water. Placed in the same light and temperature conditions as other cuttings, roots may or may not develop. The process can take from a couple of weeks to a couple of months. As soon as any root appears, a small amount of fertilized water can be added.

We go to a little more trouble because we prefer that the cutting not rest on the bottom of the glass. The simple solution is to use a small-sized

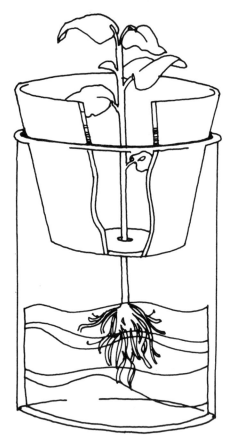

Water propagation of a stem cutting

clear plastic glass and to set inside it a party glass made of compressed plastic foam with a hole cut in the bottom. The inner container is somewhat larger than the outer, leaving a space between the two bottoms. Poke the cutting through the hole of the inner container. It will be held above the bottom of the outer glass. Some people take a piece of heavy cardboard, cut a hole in the center, and place it over a glass. The cutting goes through the hole.

When a substantial amount of root has been formed, cut away the bottom of the inner container so as not to harm the roots trying to pull them through the hole. Because the water-soaked roots have no soil to cling to, they usually stick together, forming thin bundles. Don't handle them with your fingers. Allow them to dry in the air for a few minutes, following which a good blast of breath usually blows them apart. Once the roots are somewhat spread out, plant the cutting in soilless mix, being careful to fill all the spaces in the pot. In doing so, apply as little pressure as possible in the region of the roots. Then water well and watch that the cutting never dries out.

It is worth mentioning here that there are special water propagators on the market. They consist of a glass bowl and a considerable number of small glass balls. The balls support cuttings in the water. The only advantage is aesthetic.

SUCCULENT PROPAGATION

Succulents are plants that live in deserts where the rainfall is less than 10 inches a year and the surface of the soil dries out very rapidly. Because of their sensitivity to rot from even small amounts of standing moisture, many cacti and succulents must be given special handling. All of them go through some period of dormancy during the year, the majority doing so in winter. This dormancy is of varying degrees, with some plants continuing partial activity and others becoming absolutely quiescent. Some people prefer taking cuttings only during dormancy. That requires absolute dryness until the cutting spontaneously starts to grow, whereupon light watering can start. We favor trying to root cuttings during the growing period.

There are a number of succulents that grow in relatively moist conditions and can be propagated in open containers with slightly moist vermiculite or in packaged soilless mix in the same way as other tropical plants. Knowing whether a succulent responds to a dry or moist treatment is important for successful rooting.

Pereskia, epiphyllums and *Rhipsalis* root in the usual way during their growing season. Even some plants that belong to very drought-resistant species perform normally. *Aptenia cordifolia* is one; others are Orbeas (Stapelias) and their relatives, branching Euphorbias, and Kalanchoes. These propagate easily in moderately dry soil by the open method.

However, sections of columnar cactus and stem cuttings of many leaf succulents such as Crassulas, Cotyledons, caudex (thick stemmed) Euphorbias, desert Pelargoniums (Geraniums) and others must be given a bone-dry, very porous medium. Half and half perlite and vermiculite is a good soil for the purpose; pure gritty sand or bird gravel (without seeds) are alternatives. You can use a regular soilless mix (2-1-1), provided the amount of soil is reduced to half so that it will dry out very rapidly. Another precaution is to use baked clay containers or ordinary clay pots because they dry quickly in the house.

Press the cutting, dusted at the tip with hormone powder, into the dry medium. Set in Partial Sunlight or within 3 inches of the fluorescent tubes at the center. These cuttings do require more light at this stage than most plants. Spray the cuttings lightly, morning and evening. Rooting is often slow but fairly reliable. Remember that the cutting of a succulent of this type (from the most arid deserts) will not die soon from total lack of water, but will rot quickly if it has too much. After the plant has begun to grow, it can be transferred to regular cactus-succulent mix.

LEAF CUTTINGS

Virtually the only plants that can be propagated by leaf cuttings are gesneriads, African Violets and their relatives, and Begonias. But that covers a very large number of plants, so this method of propagation is worth describing.

After the leaves of some gesneriads and all juicy-stalked Begonias are severed at the joint, cut off any *excess* length of stalk longer than one half inch. Prepare a propagating box with cover, just as for stem cuttings, using moist vermiculite as soil. Dip the end of the stalk into hormone powder, then poke it into the soil so that the base of the leaf touches it. Cover the box and treat just like a stem cutting with regard to light and temperature.

Usually a single plant develops near the joint of leaf blade and stalk. But with African Violets, there may be several little plants closely packed together. These should be allowed time to grow roots of their own and then be separated with a very narrow-bladed knife so that each plantlet has both leaf and root. Transplant temporarily to another propagation box where they will have more room between them. Finally, when they have developed a good crown, they can be potted up separately.

Begonia leaves are often so large that they make very unwieldy cuttings. You can, for one thing, cut the leaf down until there is no more than an inch above the stalk. This is quite sufficient for propagation. The remainder of the leaf can be cut into wedges that include the mid-rib, rolled as you would to make a paper funnel, and planted with the point downward in the vermiculite. This is a little more ticklish than growing

AFRICAN VIOLET LEAF

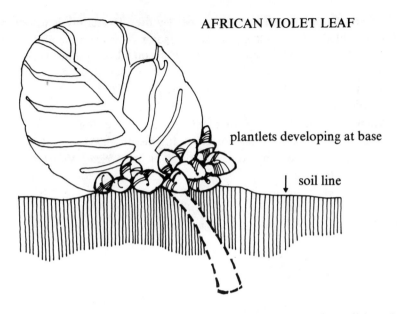

plantlets developing at base

↓ soil line

from stalk and leaf blade. Unless you maintain very good conditions for root growth, the stalked pieces will come through more often. But, usually, even a beginner will have some successes with the furled blades.

BEGONIA LEAF

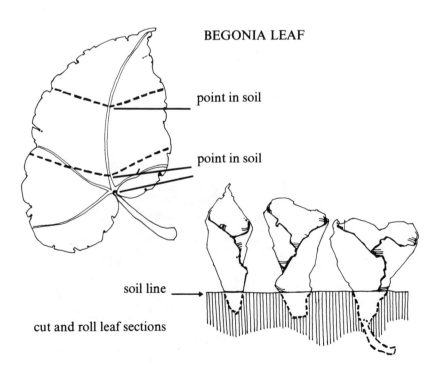

point in soil

point in soil

soil line

cut and roll leaf sections

A method that is used by some experts quite successfully is to retain the whole blade. Cut small slashes across major veins from the underside of the leaf. Lay the whole blade bottom down on a bed of moist vermiculite and pin it in place with hairpins. Dust the underside of cut veins, as well as the stalks of leaves, with hormone powder to prevent infections and probably aid rooting.

When removing leaves from plants for use as cuttings, you do not want to ruin the plant's appearance. Taking healthy leaves low down on a stem or branch, or one from the rings of an African Violet rosette causes least damage.

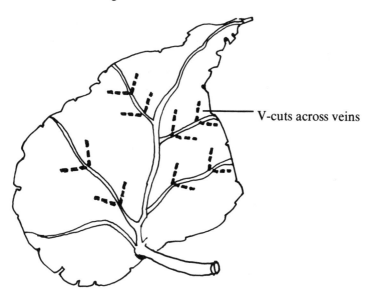

V-cuts across veins

Begonia leaf (bottom view)

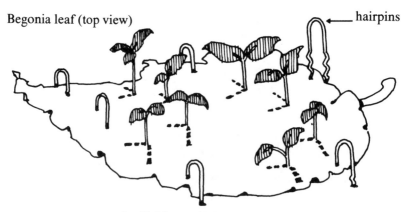

Begonia leaf (top view)

hairpins

leaf laid on soil, bottom side down

Mallet Cuts and Heel Cuts. Mallet cutting is a method used with plants having rather thick stems or branches, and widely spaced joints. This method utilizes only a single joint and a leaf. Simply make a slice on either side of a joint. If there is a leaf on either side of the joint, one of these is removed. Then plant the piece of stem horizontally in vermiculite, with the top just showing above the surface and with the leaf standing straight up.

When a plant has thick stems or branches but removing either of these is undesirable, the heel cut is sometimes used. Starting just above a joint with a leaf or a small twig, make a cut downward with a sharp, thin knife. The cut should angle inward, near-to but not reaching the center of the stem. The slice should then go past the joint and outward again. The cutting is planted in vermiculite with just the leaf exposed. The stem or branch of the parent plant is not severely damaged.

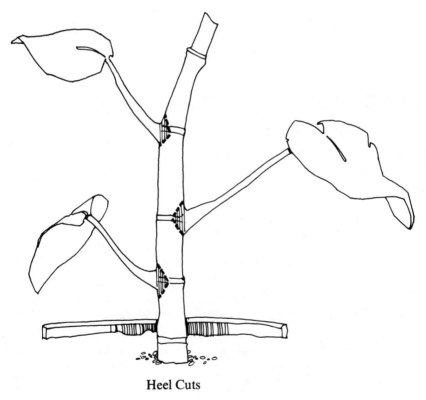

Heel Cuts

cut should not reach center of stem

DIVISION

Division is one of the most satisfactory and safest means of propagating. It is useful with two kinds of plants, those that produce baby plants at their bases in the normal course of their growth cycle (many succulents do this) and those that spread by underground roots near the surface, sending up foliage at intervals (as do, for instance, Spider Plants).

We call the baby plants offsets, or pups. Do not separate these as soon as they appear. Be patient and let them grow for a while until they have roots of their own. Then it will be easy to cut them free from the parent with a sharp thin knife and with a narrow trowel, lift out the roots. Once free, pot them up separately.

Plants that spread by means of their root system should be examined from above. You will then see the separate clumps or tufts. With a sharp knife cut these sections apart. Carefully lift each one out with a narrow trowel and pot up. Plants removed in this way almost invariably survive.

SOIL LAYERING

Soil layering is a different and simpler matter indoors than out. In the garden and orchard, it is usually a way of propagating bushes and small trees. In the house, it can be useful in multiplying almost any of the trailing plants. Usually, however, people think of it as a method useful with stolons.

A stolon is a sort of suckering branch that grows without joints and bears at its tip a cluster of leaves and sometimes flowers. This tip is also equipped to put down roots rapidly whenever it touches moist soil, for it is one of the ways in which the plant propagates itself. Typical stolons are those of Episcias, Strawberry Begonias and Spider Plants.

You can take the end of one of these stolons and, if there is free soil space in the pot, curl it back and fix it firmly in the soil with a hairpin. The hairpin should be pressed into the soil just behind the cluster of leaves. If the plant is in a small pot, and there is room for such an operation, set several pots filled with moist mix around the plant and pin a stolon into each of them. When the cluster of leaves starts to grow actively, it means the tip is rooted and you can cut it free from the parent plant. Failure only occurs if the junior pots are not kept moist.

Plants that are prolific sources of stolons can be exploited in this way to produce numerous small plants reliably and quickly.

SOIL LAYERING: Spider Plant stolons in individual pots

AIR LAYERING

Indoor growers rarely use this method except for large fig plants and Dieffenbachias. A first requirement is that the plant be rather thick-stemmed. This method produces a good-sized plant immediately, and it is the only way of topping some plants while insuring that you will have a young plant in good shape. But, before you do an air layering, consider whether you want to lose the top of the parent stem or branch, since roots are produced on the upper part of a branch or stem and everything above the cut is removed.

Starting between two nodes, drive an extremely sharp and thin knife upward part way into a stem or branch. The cut has to be long enough to be lifted somewhat, yet not so deep that the top of the stem topples over.

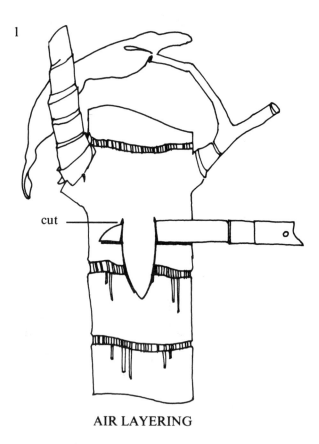

AIR LAYERING

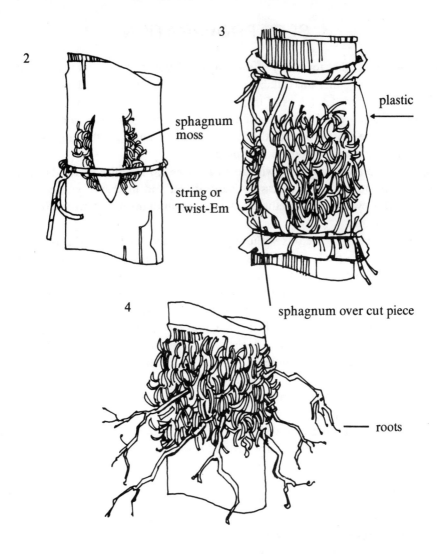

2

3

sphagnum
moss

plastic

string or
Twist-Em

4

sphagnum over cut piece

roots

Dust the wound with hormone powder. Pack moist milled sphagnum moss or peat moss into the space created by the cut. Tie the cut piece down firmly with soft cotton string or a Twist-Em.

Have another small wad of moss handy and also a square of light-weight plastic sheeting. Place the moss over the wounded part and wrap the plastic around the stem or branch very neatly, with some overhang top and bottom. Then tie top and bottom very tightly with adhesive tape, soft string or Twist-Ems to create a completely airtight bandage.

If the job has been done properly and the plant is healthy and grow-ing, you can remove the bandage in about six weeks and find a good-sized root system. The stem can be cut off with the roots and potted up.

SEED PROPAGATION

We regret that for many of the plants we would like to recommend as gifts, seed is either unavailable or relatively difficult to find. By diligently writing for seed catalogs of tropicals and house plants, you will at times discover sources that otherwise are available only to wholesale buyers. Seed is the most economical way to propagate, but it is often a slow and relatively unreliable one in the house.

As a planter, any box will do as long as it has holes in the bottom in order to get rid of excess moisture if wet and to absorb water when dry. Our own favorite method is the exception to the use of holes. Here is how it works.

Use a plastic shoe box without holes. Moisten finely sieved 2-1-1 soil-less mix or a packaged soilless mix that does not contain fertilizer. Stir water in slowly so that the soil is just moist to the touch. Fill the shoe box with soil to a depth of 1½ inches and smooth the top surface. Sprinkle the seed on top—evenly if small seed or in rows if larger. Cover with a very thin blanket of dry milled sphagnum moss. Close the box and place it so that the top is within 3 inches of the fluorescent tubes or in Bright Reflected light. The temperature must be 72 to 80 degrees F. If it is lower, set the box on a strand or two of heating cable.

With the closed box method, you don't have to worry about watering even if the seeds do not germinate for two or three months.

You can also use a box with holes in the bottom. This has the disadvantage that the soil may dry out and it will be necessary to water from the bottom—which can lead to excess moisture.

For small quantities of seed, you can use the bottom of a milk carton, a plastic cocktail glass or a plastic pot. Just cover it with a sheet of clear plastic.

Everybody has a best way of distributing small seeds. A good one is to put the dry milled sphagnum you will use as a top dressing in a bowl. Pour in a small quantity of seed and stir thoroughly. Then spread the sphagnum on the surface of your mix. There is an element of chance here, but usually there is a fair distribution without any fuss.

You might be wondering about the use of the dried milled sphagnum moss. It absorbs moisture quickly and evenly overnight in a closed box, and helps remove any excess you have inadvertently poured in.

With larger seeds, you can wait to transplant the seedlings until they have four real leaves. And, when plants from small seeds come up uncrowded, you can do the same. However, if the seedlings are massed, we like to give them room as soon as they are up. As you know, the first two leaves are cotyledons, not true leaves. Yet it is at this stage that we find it easiest to move the little plants, before they become still more jammed together through growing—that is, provided you can see what you are doing.

We use an Optivisor, which is a headband with built-in magnifying lenses that you can buy at any art shop, or a hand-held magnifying glass. As an instrument to remove the seedlings, a pair of eyebrow tweezers is ideal. Plunge the two points into the soil on either side of the plantlet and try to bring it out with some soil and root. If you keep your grip, you can then plunge it into the soil of another box or a pot, provided the soil is not packed hard.

From this point on, the culture is the same as for larger plants except that, for the first weeks, the tops of the plants should be as close to the fluorescent tubes as possible, or in good window light.

Large seeds sometimes present a problem, too. Many of the tropical ones are encased in very hard, brittle skins. Usually it is wise to file the side of the seed until you have a small hole down to the meat of the seed. Then soak overnight starting with lukewarm water. You'll find that the seed will germinate more quickly.

Generally speaking, large seeds are planted just below the surface of the soil. The depth is not as important as suggested by some growers.

Cuttings have been transplanted from the prop box to plastic cups. Later on they will be replanted in larger ceramic or plastic pots.

Putting Your Best Pot Forward With a Plant Gift

It is almost impossible to wrap plants the way you can other gifts. The ribbons, the boxes, the tissue paper that provide layers of anticipatory unwrapping are missing. A plant, no matter how you try to disguise it, reveals itself. But, while you can't hide the identity of a plant gift, you can enhance it, and that is something that doesn't work with the usual presents.

You will want to groom your plant well, of course. A little trimming here and there, removing damaged leaves or tired flowers, makes a big difference in appearance. But all that will not help a plant to look its best unless you are also careful in choosing a container to match it. The proper pot is like a well-tailored suit or a beautiful dress. Dress up your plant and you will double its attractions.

Any plant benefits from decorative potting, and there are an infinite number of ways that this can be done. Standard commercial containers on the market come in numerous shapes and designs and are made from a wide variety of materials. And every season we witness the introduction of still newer styles. Thus, anyone with good taste and ingenuity has available ample material with which to create wonderfully good-looking or amusing settings for plant gifts.

It can be argued that a very fine foliage plant or one that is in the full flush of blooming is enough in itself to please anyone as a gift. No doubt many growers pay little attention to the choice of a pot. Yet we think that care in this regard adds a new dimension to giving and enhances the feeling that the gift has involved a sincere desire to please. This is as true of smaller plants for the beginner as it is for the intermediate or expert grower. The plants in our list of recommendations are not always the showiest ones in the world, but they all will look superior in containers carefully selected to give prominence to their best features. The appeal of even the smallest plants at a benefit sale table is greatly increased when the plants are potted in an unconventional way.

The container can relate a plant gift to any interest, from shell collecting to mathematics or history. If the choice is made with sensitivity and imagination, it can prove a sensational success. Humor is also an aspect you should not ignore. Situations abound where an amusing container is ideal. The market is full of novelty containers that are droll or downright funny.

You must try to match the pot and plant to the decorative setting. That isn't always easy, for all of us tend to pick the styles we like ourselves. We love Japanese-style, matte-brown bonsai pots as well as the blue or ivory glazed ware, but, however well they may suit a given plant, they don't look right with many traditional styles of decoration. A majolica or French millefleur cache-pot will horrify someone whose home is ultra-modern. A casual gift can look pretentious in an expensive pot.

As you can see, there are all sorts of pitfalls to be avoided in present-ing plants in special containers. But if you get into the habit of thinking in terms of a plant-container-person relationship, you will soon develop the knack of doing the right and fitting thing without involving yourself in a frenzy of searching and making decisions.

Your special efforts won't be ignored. Some of our friends are known for their success in making a neat match of plant and pot. Their gifts are always a pleasure, and arouse curiosity and excitement even when in the simplest wrapping. Other acquaintances, more clumsy or careless, are recognized as the perfunctory donators which they are. So don't imagine this aspect of plant gift giving to be a small matter. The pot is nearly as important as the plant itself.

CACHE-POTS

Everybody understands the uses of pots and recognizes that an art pot can do more for a plant than a commercial clay one. But the merits of cache-pots are not so well understood.

Cache-pots, or pot holders, have always been used as a means of retaining growing plants in serviceable pots when using them in a deco-rative situation. They offer very definite advantages. It is, for instance, not usual to have a large collection of art pots for growing plants because of expense and inconvenience. Plants are constantly growing and require periodic repotting. This is a simple matter if we use standard sizes of clay or plastic pots, but stocking all the proper shapes and sizes in art pottery is far more difficult. As plants grow, they have different potential deco-rative uses. For instance, a medium-size plant may look fine as the cen-terpiece of a dinner table. Six months later it may be too big for this purpose and will look better on a side table. The decorative scheme having changed, a different pot is called for. With a small collection of cache-pots, you can switch from plant to plant according to size and location in the decorative scheme. It is also difficult to handle very large

Several styles of ceramic cache-pots.

plants in an art pot because of weight, while a clay pot or a plastic one can be set in a lightweight cache-pot.

With the exception of Japanese pots that have a classic beauty and are adapted to special decorative uses, it is far easier to dress up a plant in an ordinary pot with a handsome, amusing or useful cache-pot (pot cover) than to pot it up directly in an art pot. Although there are a great many styles of pots, the range of cache-pots, both intended for the purpose and adapted, is even greater. Because the cache-pot is pure container and does not need to hold soil, many more materials can be used—besides pottery and china and plastic there are straw and other fibers, wood, metal, glass, cork, stone and tree fern.

A pot does not have to fit perfectly into a cache-pot. Of course the plant must look right in proportion and form. But if the pot is too small, fill in the extra space with plastic pebbles, coarse sand, sphagnum moss or any other material that looks right.

PLASTIC POTS and CACHE-POTS

We recommend plastic pots over clay for growing indoors because they are lighter, take up less space, are superior in retaining moisture and offer a less comfortable home for insects. We also find them superior to

83

other types of pots. Very lightweight plastic foam, for example, is unpleasant to look at and handle, very breakable and top-heavy. Nurseries and florists often sell plants in a very thin, somewhat flexible plastic pot with holes at the base on the side of the pot rather than beneath it. These are unsuitable as gift containers and the plant should always be repotted in something more substantial.

Standard plastic pots of good quality. Neat and adequate.

Standard thin, hard plastic pots come in both round and square shapes. The rounds range in size from 2 to over 10 inches in diameter. They come in standard depths either the same or slightly shorter than the diameter, and also in so-called azalea pot form, which is half as deep. Square plastic pots are available from 2 inches to 4 inches in diameter, but are not available in larger sizes.

Standard colors are white or green. "Utility color" is also often specified and means a nondescript, generally grayish mixture. Our favorite color is terra cotta, which looks very neat and is almost equivalent to the traditional clay pot color. Unfortunately, this color turns up only occasionally on the market, usually in the 2- to 5-inch sizes.

These thin, hard plastic pots are adequate for indoor growing, for holding small gift plants, or as containers for benefit plant sale tables. But they do nothing to "dress up" the plant. When that is desirable you must seek other types of containers.

Designer pots, made of heavier plastic in decorator colors, ornamented or plain, start with a diameter of 4 inches. A common feature in the more modern styles is a built-in reservoir for water and a clip-on saucer. But other styles have no provision for a saucer and often lack holes in the bottom as they are intended for use as cache-pots rather than for plants with soil.

There are a bewildering number of plastic designs on the market that run the gamut of national styles. There are, for instance, colorful facsim-

For a special Holiday present, fill a Venetian glass bowl with golden Cockscomb, which will continue to grow and bloom for the rest of the winter.

Interesting ways of planting African Violets are always in demand. Here, a large Horse Conch is the planter and a handsome decorative object in itself.

Big or little, a Parsley Aralia looks its best in a fine glazed pot. The small rooted cutting makes a charming hostess present. Or try making several arrangements for a fund-raising boutique.

Pilea, Asparagus Fern and frilly Boston Fern in pots arranged in a shallow bonsai container. Moistened long fiber sphagnum moss is packed around them. Use a variety of plant materials to make a lovely housewarming gift in minutes.

A decorated glass bowl sets off this *Aglaonema* 'Silver Queen' to perfection. A charming gift for all occasions.

Three pots of easily grown Wax Begonias, placed in a rust-stained grape basket, become a centerpiece gift for the birthday girl or boy.

A handsome variegated miniature Geranium in a simple Japanese pot.

It's easy to make holes in feather rock (from builders' supply stores) and create a miniature rock garden or a pot for a single plant. This arrangement is supported on a plastic stand.

An exhibit of recycled containers. Even an old sneaker will do for a teen-ager or for a tennis buff.

A Chinese tea can makes a decorative cache-pot for a young *Begonia aconitifolia.* A lovely gift for an intermediate grower.

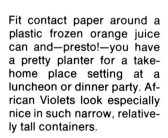

Fit contact paper around a plastic frozen orange juice can and—presto!—you have a pretty planter for a take-home place setting at a luncheon or dinner party. African Violets look especially nice in such narrow, relatively tall containers.

Plant small-leaved Fittonia in silvered metal champagne glasses as place setting gifts for the wedding party dinner.

This Swedish Ivy, *Plectranthus oertendahlii,* grows and blooms comfortably in a plain shallow baked saucer. A lovely centerpiece for the party table.

Even a porcelain Harlequin pot can be used as a temporary cache-pot for this delicate *Nephrolepis* 'Norwoodii'.

A plastic umbrella-shaped container filled with Marigolds makes an appropriate shower present or centerpiece.

Grow Crossandra indoors all year round. Here it is in an inexpensive modern cache-pot, all ready for a special gift-giving occasion.

The gold-veined Oxalis (*O. martiana aureo-reticulata*) makes a beautiful and carefree gift.

Cast ceramic frog is well designed to hold a large rooted plant such as this *Kalanchoe* 'Fireball'. Perfect for a friend with a patio or terrace garden.

Constant trimming turns a Rosemary plant into an artistic small tree. Give it at a farewell party for a close friend or business associate—"Rosemary for remembrance."

The tawny color of the pot cover exactly suits this sprawling, beautiful Geranium, *Pelargonium* 'Dr. Livingston', a delightfully sweet-smelling variety. A great gift for a beginner.

iles of American and Mexican Indian pottery and of flamboyant Italian decoration. Handsome shapes are produced in brilliant white, or white is used as a background for various colorful figures, traditional or modern.

You can grow plants directly in any of these pots, even those without holes. To provide proper drainage for the soil, make holes in the bottom of the pot with a round, pointed tool heated to the melting point of the plastic.

A cache-pot is simply a decorative container for a pot and has the advantage that it can be changed at will according to your decorative needs. The only thing you have to watch is that water does not accumulate in the bottom. But it is easy enough to pour it out after a watering. It is often easier to use a cache-pot than to transplant from a plain to a decorative pot, and there is the additional gain that the recipient of a gift can use the cache-pot for other plants and indeed constantly reuse it. Plastic cache-pots are neither as permanent nor as aesthetic as those made of pottery and are not to be considered as individual pieces of artistic merit. But they do have considerable practical value in dressing up plants at no great expense.

Local stores do not carry all the lines of plastic put out by the different manufacturers—mail-order houses have even fewer. The only thing to do is to shop thoroughly and investigate fully the kinds of plastic pots that are available in your area. Patio furniture sections of department stores sometimes carry the finer ware, and garden centers are always a possibility. Stores specializing in giftware are also worth visiting. Not infrequently, variety stores come up with interesting plastic pots.

TERRA COTTA POTS

Terra cotta is a low-fired red or tan clay from which most commercial flower pots are made. Don't confuse it with stoneware or china—they are fired at higher temperatures. Terra cotta is porous, which makes it excellent for growing in a greenhouse or out-of-doors. Indoors, it has several disadvantages—it is heavy, takes up a lot of room, is hard to clean, and soil tends to dry out rapidly. Clay pots can be used for top-heavy plants, but the saucer for the pot cannot be of terra cotta if it is to stand on shelving or furniture, because it will sweat any water it contains. The saucer must be of plastic.

The classic nursery pot with its broad, thick collar has a more natural look than plastic, but is certainly no beauty. A simple outward-curving style without a thickened rim looks far better. Such pots can be found occasionally in the shops. A novelty potter makes attractive straight-sided cubes that are an interesting break with tradition.

A fine display of small pots for plants by an art potter.

Unglazed hand thrown pottery, although never labelled as such, is often no more than terra cotta. Hand thrown or formed pots can be either just as clumsy as any commercial pot or very much more beautiful. One should be choosy. Local potters are often willing to make pots to your specifications in quite small numbers. If well designed, terra cotta pots can be as fine as any others.

JAPANESE-STYLE POTS

We call these pots Japanese-style pots rather than bonsai pots because they are not all used for bonsai and we don't want to give the impression that every pot of this type is Japanese-made. Japanese pots of every shape, size and finish have been copied by potters in this country and elsewhere. It is the uniqueness of their style—the fact that they are immediately recognizable as different from the pots of any other country—that makes Japanese pots so very popular and widely imitated.

The Japanese tradition has evolved containers in simple shapes and colors which have an earthy quality that blends beautifully with the colors and textures of greenery. The ware is all rather low-fired and gritty, with a finish or glaze on the outside and the plain porous bisque inside. The basic Japanese-style pot color is a dark brown which is not so much a glaze as a coating of finer clay that has been colored and smoothed until it glows. The forms are simple and geometrical, but much more varied than our commercial European-American clay pots. In addition, there is a wide range of shapes, some with molded designs on the surface, that are glazed in traditional gray or blue shades. Western copies of all these pots often err in trying to make them more decorative and end up with finishes and shapes that don't look nearly as well in use.

These wonderful Japanese pots are ideal for anything from a tiny plant through broad shallow plantings. As big cylindrical tubs or cache-pots, they set off a large plant to its best advantage. However, though splendid in themselves, they do not always blend with all styles of decoration. When planning a gift using this ware, don't forget to consider whether it will fit in the decorative scheme in which it will be placed.

Good Japanese pots can be used over and over again and are welcome gifts along with the plants.

GLAZED POTTERY, STONEWARE and PORCELAIN

There is very good news for indoor growers. Makers of higher-fired ware—stoneware and porcelain—are no longer treating their products as if they were only intended for cache-pots; manufacturers are now putting holes in the bottoms. Without holes, it is very difficult to grow plants in internally glazed pots. You can put drainage material in the bottom before filling with soil, but it remains very difficult to determine the amount of water to give a plant in order to satisfy its needs and still stay short of flooding the bottom. Now that high-fired ware has holes, you can take advantage of the many beautiful shapes and glazes that are available.

It is in glazed ceramic ware that you find the greatest variety of pot shapes covering every known traditional and modern style. Many can be used as cache-pots; the ones in lattice work decoration can only be used in that way.

You can also find amusing animal shapes with space for planting. One porcelain manufacturer has pure white containers in such shapes as paper bags, pickle-cartons (or coleslaw) and berry baskets. They're without holes, but are charming temporary homes for plants and lasting gifts in themselves.

Almost any glazed container can be turned into a planter. Consider large pitchers and wash bowls. They are available new or in antique shops. Creamers, cow creamers, coffee cups, mugs (coffee and beer), sugar bowls, crocks, gelatin molds, tureens, mixing bowls, old tea pots without the lids, etc. are really fun to plant in.

Ceramic pots are more readily available than plastic ones in department, gift and furniture stores. There are few communities that do not offer a curious shopper examples of ware that can be turned into handsome or amusing gift potting for plants.

All of these pots can be used for gifts with plants. From a potter's studio.

FEATHER ROCK

Feather rock is a lava stone that is anything but featherweight. But it is both lighter and more easily worked than most other stone materials. With a chisel or even a screwdriver, you can carve out holes in a few minutes. The gray, blackish or brownish material comes in chunks of various sizes. Depending on the project, you can shape these chunks and make holes for one or several plants. Builder's supply outlets throughout the country stock this material. Pick out the shapes you prefer or buy large pieces to cut or break up.

Usually, plants and their soil are planted directly in the holes. The use of pots is made difficult by the problem of shaping the holes exactly. But you can make removal and substitution of plants much easier by decanting your plant into a plastic bag with a hole or two in the bottom. Trim any excess sheet and fit it into the scooped out hollow.

Very interesting plantings can be made with this rock, especially when you use trailers or succulents. The finished composition should be set on a slab of wood or on a tray that is a suitable match. Together, rock and stand make splendid gift pieces.

CORK

Natural cork bark has been used effectively in making the sides of picturesque pots and cache-pots with bottoms consisting of other materials. Sheet cork forms an effective decorative surface for round and square pedestals.

TREE FERN

Tree fern trunks are brown or black and when dried are very light, porous, and brittle-spongy in structure and feel. They make splendid baskets or pots for orchids and for the more showy branching-trailing plants, especially ferns. Because water drains right through them, it is best to hang tree fern containers over a tiled surface, or to dip them periodically, along with their contents, in water.

Tree fern is also used frequently in the form of poles and slabs for training foliage vines.

Straw-covered pedestals in the foreground, mirror-covered ones in back. Platforms inside support the plant.

STRAW and OTHER BASKET MATERIALS

Recently, there has been a great increase in the popularity of baskets for a variety of decorative uses. They are being imported from all over the world in increasing quantities and in some surprising and beautiful designs. Round and square baskets of all sizes make fine cache-pots. But we would prefer to use only the less elegant ones unless it is understood that the recipient of the gift will remove the pot and use the basket. Unfortunately, damage is inevitable if fine pieces are used with a potted plant for a long period of time. Line the basket with plastic sheeting, sewing it on the inside along the top edge. For a unique gift, treat a straw hat the same way. Wicker and many other by-products of plant origin are used by basket makers, and the sturdier kinds can be both durable and handsome as cache-pots.

WOOD

Wood tubs for large plants are made of ordinary pine, of oak and of other woods. The softer woods, which are more liable to decay, must be painted inside with a coat of creosote-based paint if they are to be used for potting. Others are sufficiently decay resistant. Yet we hate to use wooden tubs at all for potting, especially the more expensive and handsomer ones. We recommend employing them as cache-pots with large plastic pots inside.

METAL

Metal is not often used for pots because it is subject to corrosion from soil chemicals. Exceptions are copper or brass pots that are expensive but often very handsome. Nowadays, these are usually bought as antiques. A fine old metal jardiniere, tea caddy or biscuit box may serve as a splendid cache-pot.

Metal is also used to form most of the pedestals for plants. These are essentially tubes of different lengths with a platform inside holding a saucer. Pedestals come in chrome finish and with various coverings such as cork, adhesive plastic (such as Con-Tact paper), bamboo, plastic finishes, matting, etc. Pedestals are useful for the display of individual plants at different heights. The gift of plant and pedestal together is another way of dressing up a plant for presentation.

PLANTERS as GIFTS

A planter is an open container in which several plants are arranged in their pots. It can be put together in a matter of minutes and changed around at will. It is one way to make a plant present "important" using small plants and a good-looking container. It makes a fine dining table centerpiece or a temporary arrangement displayed on a side table. The idea is useful at any time and can be practiced for your own pleasure before venturing to create gifts.

The planter should be of glass, wood, ceramic or any material that comes as a square or rectangular form 6 inches long or more. We often use a large Japanese brown bonsai planter that is 8x12x3 inches high. The sides should always be equal to or higher than the depth of the pots you intend to use.

The best plants to use are small trailers and flowering plants, ferns, little trees or succulents. One to six plants may be used for a planter of the above-mentioned size. The pots must all be no more than 3 inches high. They are set on the bottom of the planter and sphagnum moss, sand, pebbles, plastic chips, marble chips, sheet moss or any attractive filler material is packed around them. The filler material can rise in the center of the planter, covering any pots that are the same height as the planter itself. Care only involves watering the pots and keeping the arrangement in sufficient light when not on display.

MAKING YOUR OWN DECORATIVE CONTAINERS

WASTEBASKETS

Straw, fiber or metal decorative wastebaskets make elegant homes for plants on a temporary basis. Fill with an appropriately large foliage plant. The basket dresses up the plant and vice versa. Of course, it is not meant as a permanent cache-pot.

PAINTING POTS

Decorate white painted clay pots. They are usually available in the stores, but if you can't find any, do the job yourself with acrylic or porcelain paint. Stencil a leaf or stylized flower design on the sides, or paint cross-hatched lines to simulate lattice work. There are, of course, endless numbers of designs that can either be stencilled or painted to provide decoration.

An old sneaker makes a rakish and amusing cache-pot for a small plant.

BIRD CAGES

Oriental bird cages made of bamboo or reed are not very expensive. They make lovely homes for vines, trailing plants or ferns. The more elegant metal ones are perfect settings for a big present.

WOODEN TUBS

Wrap a small wooden tub with twisted raffia to fit sides and bottom. Paint with clear polyurethane or clear nail polish. Make a knotted rope hanger. Fit a plastic pot saucer inside the tub. Place plant and pot inside the tub.

BEER and SODA CANS

Beer and soft drink cans are of light metal sprayed with polyurethane plastic inside. Punch holes in the bottom. Decorate with adhesive plastic (such as Con-Tact paper) and use as flower pots.

METAL CANS

Tea cans and many others of the same type are colored and decorated with picturesque designs. Spray or paint the interior with clear polyurethane plastic, which can be purchased at any hardware or paint store. Punch holes in the bottom. Use as amusing pots. If the can has a small opening, cut along edge with a can opener. Canisters can be treated in the same fashion.

FLEXIBLE PLASTIC CONTAINERS

Bleach, detergent and other bottles can be cut quite evenly with a hot knife. Sandpaper the edge until it is even. Poke holes in the bottom with a heated ice pick. Paint the container with a bright color and use as a pot.

A recycled silvered glass perfume bottle top makes a truly elegant setting for a small Table Fern. Make more of them as favors for a celebration.

Mango. *Mangifera indica.*

Labeling and Transporting Plant Gifts

LABELING for NAME
and CULTURAL DIRECTIONS

Every plant gift should be accompanied by a label bearing its name unless you are certain that the person receiving it already knows it. Expert growers are familiar with the names of their plants, but beginners and intermediates usually only know the common names.

In regard to most plants, the common name you happen to know is of no value to someone else. Seed catalogs are full of common names for plants, but if you compare them in different catalogs, you will find very little uniformity. That is because most of these names are not really common. Properly speaking, a common name should be one that everybody applies to a plant. In the U.S., everyone calls *Tagetes* a Marigold—so that's a good common name. But when nurserymen invent names for unfamiliar plants, nothing is accomplished but confusion. Even cactus has become a common name and we see variety stores labeling any succulent "Cactus."

At plant society meetings we are showered with questions about ailing plants. If the plant has been left at home, the first thing we have to do is find out its name. When we ask this question, the answer usually is "I don't know" or something like "the Busybee Plant." Since we don't know the Busybee Plant, we ask for a description. Nine times out of ten, the reply is so general that it is of no help at all.

So, if you do not label a plant with its correct name, you are preparing future trouble for the recipient. If any problem arises, there is no way of tracing down the identity of the plant except by showing it to an expert. There is no harm in using common names in conversation between people who agree about which plant they are discussing. We even use them in our plant list. But your label *must* bear the correct name—and that is no other than the botanical Latin designation.

Common names change from country to country and sometimes from state to state in the U.S.A. But Latin is the universal language of plants.

The name applied by botanists is understood in Japan, Russia, Germany, the United States—indeed, everywhere.

The Latin name consists of two parts, a generic name and a species name. The generic name states the kind of plant it is—for instance *Rosa, Viola, Begonia*. The species name tells you which kind of *Rosa, Viola* or *Begonia* it is. *Rosa blanda* is a particular kind of wild rose. *Rosa rugosa* is a different one. The species name is often descriptive.

There is a third kind of name called the cultivar name. That is the one given to a particular plant in cultivation. The generic name is often only followed by the cultivar name. So we can have *Aglaonema commutatum* 'Silver Queen' or *Sinningia* 'Freckles', 'Dollbaby' and 'Cindy'. They aren't species any more but cultivated plants. Begonias have as many cultivars as species so you have names like *Begonia prismatocarpa* and *Begonia* 'Tingley Mallet'.

To be completely helpful, therefore, your label must have a generic and species name or a generic and cultivar name. If you choose to add the common name, that's fine, but not necessary.

Incidentally, for many people the Latin is a pure mental block. No knowledge of the language is necessary if you treat the words just as names. We all use Rhododendron, Azalea, Calceolaria, Cyclamen, Cineraria, Delphinium, Impatiens, etc. without thinking. Adding a few more names of this kind should be no real problem.

Mail-order firms supplying plants usually attach correct Latin labels. Shops often supply plastic printed labels bearing only a common name. When buying plants, save yourself trouble by insisting on the Latin name. Otherwise, you must look up the plant in a reference book, which isn't always easy. And how many people own botanical reference books?

Blank white plastic labels are very inexpensive. Write on them with a special black grease pencil or fit them with self-sticking paper labels. The self-sticking labels will adhere to the sides of plastic pots but will not stick to clay ones.

If you give a familiar plant to a competent grower, there is no need for cultural advice. An unusual plant will elicit questions about ways of handling it and you can count on such a person remembering your suggestions. Not so beginners and intermediate growers. Our experience is that verbal advice is neither completely understood nor remembered. On occasion we have given advice only to have the person reporting failure and giving us back a version of our directions which was totally unrecognizable. Memory acts best with aspects of familiar ideas, but it easily confuses new ones.

If you want a plant to survive with its new owner, you must find a way for your advice to stick. That can be done by writing up a short list of cultural directions.

The need for this kind of help is greatest at public sales. Try to make a tag—a piece of file card will do—with the necessary information: whether the plant needs much or little water, the minimum temperature that should be maintained, how often to fertilize and what kind of fertilizer to use, and how much light. That can all be stated in a few words.

TRANSPORTING GIFT PLANTS

There is no safe way to send a small or medium size gift plant a long distance in its pot because it is a certainty that it will not be transported all the way in an upright position or be spared severe jostling. Plants large enough for big pots or tubs—good sized shrubs or young trees—can be sent by truck, as the commercial nurseries do, either without packing or wrapped in burlap. But it is necessary to use a trucker accustomed to moving plants. Far better to order such gift plants from a nursery which will take the responsibility for delivery.

Smaller plants for short journeys need not be wrapped at all. A good carrier is a large shopping bag or carton, the sides well stuffed with tissue paper or styrofoam peanuts so that plant and pot are held in an upright position. Cover the top of the plant in winter with several layers of lightweight plastic. Cleaners bags are excellent for the purpose.

A neat trick with a small plant is to put it into a plastic bag, then blow air in until the branches no longer touch the sides, and close tightly with a rubber band or Twist-Em. Pack as we've described above.

Peperomia caperata 'Tricolor'.

Cultural Plant List

The plants listed in the following pages are selected because they are attractive in one way or another and are among the easiest to grow indoors. They also have one other qualification. We think that they make excellent gifts for any of the persons and purposes we discussed in earlier chapters. Although this is only a small part of the current house plant repertory, we hope that some of the plants will be a new experience for many of our readers. We trust that you will be encouraged to try other unfamiliar plants both for yourselves and as gifts.

Each description consists of two parts. In the first we sometimes describe the appearance of the plant when it is not too well known and recommend ways of growing it. The second part is reserved for a more general discussion, sometimes centering around the plant's usefulness as a gift, sometimes mentioning special virtues and special problems.

Beneath the name of each plant you will find three short phrases that give you some important information in a glance. The first phrase tells the type of grower for whom the plant is most appropriate. Line 2 tells for which occasion the plant is *especially* suited, and the third line gives the most successful method of propagation.

AFRICAN VIOLET. *Saintpaulia.*

Beginners, young people
Party favors, benefits, hospital gifts
Leaf cuttings

The African Violet needs no introduction. We grow it in 2-1-1 soilless mix with 2 tablespoons of lime chips or crushed eggshell added. Keep it moderately moist at over 65 degrees F. and fertilize with a formula having a very high phosphate number—usually specially labelled for the plant. Light requirement varies, but Partial Sun or up to a foot under fluorescent light is usually sufficient. Propagation is by leaf cuttings as descibed on pages 70-71. The best varieties may be considered beginners' plants.

****

A miniature African Violet plant fits neatly into the opening of a large Florida Horse Conch. Shells make lovely temporary pots that later on can be treated as table ornaments.

The problem with African Violets as gifts is that they are so popular that many indoor growers quite unjustly disdain them and African Violet hobbyists, who are legion, are so knowledgeable of their own favorites that it would be hard to please them.

Still, there are always those who have never grown these plants and young people who must get to know them some time. So there do exist opportunities for giving. If you are not sure which plants to choose among the thousands of hybrids, we would like to suggest the 'Ballet Lisa' and the plants listed in the annual honor roll of the *African Violet Magazine*, compiled by Mrs. M. G. Gonzalez.

We would also like to point out that there are many mini-violets which will look adorable in bloom in small plastic terrariums or art clay pots and which will enchant as favors at parties and as items for the sale table of a benefit.

ALUMINUM PLANT. *Pilea cadierei.*

Beginners, intermediates
All occasions
Stem cuttings

This is an upright plant not more than 15 inches high, producing stiff stems and few branches and remarkable for its metallic patterned leaves.

A *pilea cadierei,* an easy-to-grow plant for beginners. Rooted cuttings are ideal for the sale table.

It is undemanding and capable of being handled by a beginning grower. Give it packaged potting soil with perlite added or 2-1-1 soilless mix. Fertilize regularly with a high nitrate formula and keep moderately moist at all times. This plant does well in a north window but benefits from Partial Sun and artificial light. Keep tops 6 inches below the tubes and temperature over 60 degrees F. Propagation is by stem cuttings in an open box or pot with soilless mix.

****

About 1½ inches long, oval, and pointed at the tip, the Aluminum Plant's leaves are quilted shallowly with zones of brilliant silver between the green veins. They are rather loosely whorled around the stem and stick out horizontally on short stalks. The plant only looks well when there are a number of stems close together, but these are freely produced from spreading underground roots. If you nip the tips of the stems, a vertical shoot grows from the joint below instead of branching. However, this nipping does encourage new stems to grow from the base.

The plants are already showy in a 2-inch pot and, by the time they are big enough to fit a 4- or 6-incher, they are worthy to be substantial gifts. Growth is quite rapid, by the way. Thus, depending on their size, you can have gifts for almost any occasion. But be wary of giving them to experts or specialist-hobbyists—they might find these plants a bit too ordinary.

BALSAM. *Impatiens balsamina.* Touch-Me-Not.

All growers
Favors, hostess gifts, benefits (in winter)
Stem cuttings, seed

Dwarf Balsams can be brought in from the garden in late summer. Since they are annuals, they may be on their last legs at that time, so it will be advisable for you to take cuttings and start new plants for winter bloom immediately. This is quicker than using seed and you can also, in this way, propagate the colors that you prefer. Cuttings root quickly in 1-1-1 soilless mix using sand instead of perlite. If you have no garden, plant seeds indoors in September for winter bloom.

Balsam needs more sun than its close relative Impatiens. Give it Full Sun at the windowsill. If the light is inadequate, the plants will lengthen and fail to flower. Under fluorescent lights, place them 3 inches below the tubes. Pot in sterilized garden soil with the addition of vermiculite and perlite or in 1-1-1 mix with sand. Fertilize with a high phosphate-potash formula. Allow these plants to dry out between waterings. If plants are kept in the window, be particularly cautious of over-watering during cloudy spells. Keep the temperature over 60 degrees F. With plants brought in from the garden, watch out for aphids and other pests and wash them off promptly.

****

Gifts of Balsam in summer are unthinkable because they are so common at that time. But indoor growers are not yet used to the idea of blooming annuals indoors, so that these handsome plants, unavailable in the winter months, arouse wonder and delight when given in the off-season. This plant can never be an important gift, but young blooming cuttings make great favors, hostess gifts and plants for the benefit sale table. Since the growth of Balsam is slow and flowering does not start up immediately, it is advisable to put down cuttings in September for December giving and in November for February or March giving.

BASIL, FRENCH. *Ocimum basilicum minimum.*

All growers
Hostess gifts, benefits (in winter)
Stem cuttings, seed

The French Basil is a small-leaved, upright-growing herb, single-stemmed and producing a number of branches. At most you will need a deep 5-inch pot for a full-grown specimen. Use 1-1-1 soilless mix or packaged potting soil with perlite added. Also add 2 to 3 tablespoons of lime chips or crushed eggshell to each quart. Keep moist at all times and fertilize with a high nitrate formula. Grow in Bright Reflected or Partial Sun or under fluorescent tubes. This plant is subject to attack by white fly and aphids, both of which can be removed by frequent washings. Maintain the temperature above 55 degrees F. Propagation is easy by means of stem cuttings in soilless mix in an open box, an enclosed box or a plastic bag.

Don't confuse this fine culinary herb with the Basil called Dark Opal. Ours is light green, the leaves no more than 1½ inches long (usually less), and the flavor, for tomatoes, salads and sauces, superb. It also makes a far neater plant in the house. Seed is now available from local seedsmen, and occasionally the plants are sold in the shops. Once you have plants, you can produce as many as you need from cuttings.

****

Basil makes a fine present in the midst of winter when even the nurseries don't have it. Seed planted in August or September and cuttings in September-October will be ready for gifts before Christmas, and will carry on well beyond this holiday. It's a wonderful hostess gift for a good cook and perfect for small presents for all kinds of parties. In winter it should be a spectacular seller at benefits.

BEGONIA, FIBROUS ROOTED.

Intermediates, specialist-hobbyists
All occasions
Stem cuttings, seed

Wax Begonias are easy to grow and bloom, but short-lived and difficult to keep in a compact shape. Rhizomatous Begonias present very real problems with watering and take a relatively long time to develop from cuttings. Fibrous Rooted Begonias are those we can recommend to an intermediate grower for sturdiness, ease of culture, handsome leaves and seasonal flowering. They are also the easiest to propagate and grow with moderate speed.

These Begonias can be kept moderately moist throughout the year, just like so many of our other tropicals. Temperature is the same, too—above 65 degrees F. Soil should be 2-1-1 soilless mix with 2 tablespoons of lime chips or crushed eggshell to the quart. Fertilize with a balanced formula. Light requirement is Partial Sun to Bright Reflected light or fluorescent. Five to 6 inches under the tubes on a 12-hour day is usually sufficient. It is unnecessary to make leaf cuttings with these plants which need trimming anyway. Stem cuttings root easily in a closed box. Seed is treated in the usual way.

The two types of Fibrous Rooted Begonias are those with canes and those that are shrubby. Cane types have long stems which do not branch much. Shrubby types are much branched.

The best of the modern Begonias are hybrids and therefore must be propagated from cuttings. However, there are some fine old species that are very vigorous. Begonia nurseries carry long lists of different kinds, both species and hybrids, with their descriptions.

The variety of leaf forms and colorings and sizes is so great that recommending some over others is purely speculative—you will have your own preferences. The hybrids of Michael Kartuz and Belva Kusler, usually indicated in the catalogs, are especially fine. Here are a few suggestions:

B. 'Di-Anna'. An old hybrid with narrow angel leaves and low growth. Salmon flowers. A good basket plant. Cane.

B. dichoroa. A cane species with large plain green leaves and orange flowers. Very sturdy.

B. 'Laura Englebert' (Kusler). Dark copper-red leaves and coral-red flowers. Stiff canes up to 3 feet.

B. 'Lenore Olivier' (Kusler). Cane. Very dark leaves, low and compact. Brilliant salmon flowers.

B. 'Miyo Berger' (Kusler). Small black leaves with pinkish-silver spots. Pink flowers. Cane, but quite dwarf.

B. 'Orange Rubra' Hybrid (Kartuz). Silver-spotted dark copper leaves. Compact cane. Orange flowers.

B. 'W. Newton'. Spreading canes for a basket. Silver-spotted leaves. Orange flowers.

Among the larger-leaved shrub Begonias are:

B. metallica. Bronze leaves, pink flowers. A climber. Very sturdy.

B. rubromarginata. Oval leaves that are red-edged. Strong upright stems. Red and white flowers.

The smaller-leaved shrub Begonias include:

B. bartonea. Medium-size light green leaves streaked with brown and silver. Small pink flowers.

B. 'Bayern'. Spreading basket plant with small bronze leaves dusted with silver. Pink flowers.

B. 'Concord' (Kartuz). Low spreading plant with whitish flowers and small, ruffled, glossy, blackish leaves.

B. foliosa. Fern Begonia. Tiny leaves on arching branches. Little white flowers. Fine for baskets.

B. fuchsioides. Trailing stems bear tiny leaves and little red flowers.

B. preussen. Compact shrubby plant with bronze leaves, pink flowers.

B. 'Sachsen'. Similar to *preussen* but more sturdy and everblooming.

****

The Fibrous Rooted Begonias are a splendid source of varied and interesting plants for propagating and giving. Look over the plants at nurseries or consult catalogs. You will find that you can select plants of just the size, growth habit and coloring that you prefer. And, except among Begonia hobbyists, you will find that very few of the hybrids are well-known. In other words, you can have unusual plants that are familiar as a type—as Begonias—yet a complete novelty in respect to the variety.

BEGONIA, REX. *Begonia.*

Intermediates, experts
All occasions
Rhizome cuttings, leaf cuttings, seed

Strictly for intermediate and expert growers, Rex Begonias are the most colorful and varied of foliage plants. On the west coast, where humidity is high and temperatures are temperate during the day but plummet at night, these plants flourish in the house. But in most of the rest of the country, conditions are less favorable.

Rex Begonias have a thick rhizome which crawls along the ground and sends down shallow roots into the soil. Watering is very critical and a slight mistake can ruin a plant. Pots have to dry out quite thoroughly between moistenings. One expert we know of makes it a rule not to water some of his Rexes until their leaves begin to sag on their stalks.

In spite of this distaste for much watering, the plants do like very high humidity and with it develop their largest leaves and finest colors. Fertilize moderately with a balanced formula. The plants do very well under fluorescent light at a distance of 12 to 18 inches and in a window with Partial Sunlight in the city and Bright Reflected light in the country.

Propagation is by seeds, which are readily available, and by rhizome cuttings and leaf cuttings.

****

There are numerous other begonias with rhizomes that are quite different from the Rexes in appearance and whose handsome hybrids are just as beautiful. But, as a group, none can compare with the Rexes in variety of coloring. While some Rex Begonias are pure beaten silver, others are zoned in concentric bands of red, silver-green or purple. The shape of the leaf is usually a broad angel wing, some being up to a foot in length and 8 inches wide.

If you can grow the Rexes, you will never lack for friends happy to have these plants—even if they do kill them in a few months. They are plants you need not be ashamed to give on the grandest of occasions— provided they are well-grown, colorful and symmetrical.

BEGONIA, WAX. *Begonia semperflorens.*
Intermediates
Christmas, Easter, party gifts, benefits
Stem cuttings

Dwarf Wax Begonias can be brought in from the garden before they have deteriorated in the fall. With trimming, they will continue to bloom indoors through part of the fall and winter if kept constantly moist and well-lighted. Cuttings started at this time will be ready for gift giving before Christmas.

Indoors, use 2-2-1 soilless mix. Even garden plants benefit from transplanting to this medium. Add lime chips or crushed eggshell to the mix. Fertilize regularly with a high phosphate-potash formula. Allow the plants to dry out somewhat between waterings.

Keep begonias in a partially sunny window or under lights at a distance of 4 inches. Cuttings root easily in moist vermiculite in an open box as long as the temperature is maintained above 65 degrees F. Seed may be planted in the fall for Christmas and spring giving. Use azalea-type pots, as the roots are spreading rather than deep.

Recommended for intermediate growers.

****

Of the Wax Begonias, choose dwarf types. The Calla Lily begonias should be avoided and single-flowered plants are better indoors than double-flowered ones. They should be constantly trimmed and groomed because the seed pods of the female flowers are unsightly and inhibit flowering.

As gifts, the plants are of little interest in the warm months, but in midwinter, when they are not seen in the shops and their flowering is most appreciated, they make nice party gifts, hostess presents and plants for benefit sales.

At times, these begonias show considerable variations in growth pattern and flowering. If you find a particularly colorful and easy plant, cherish it and root cuttings for your friends and for special occasions. At their best, Wax Begonias are delightful plants to have blooming during the cold months.

CACTUS, MISTLETOE.
Rhipsalis mesembryanthoides.

Beginners
Housewarmings, shower presents
Stem cuttings

The name Mistletoe Cactus has been applied to almost all the tubular-stemmed Rhipsalis, a group of leafless plants of the cactus family. *R. mesembryanthoides,* however, has lately been sold a good deal under this name. As for the others, the culture is much the same and they are a group you should get to know better because they are very easy to grow—a beginner can handle them. They have pretty white, yellow or pink flowers followed by long-lasting mistletoe-like berries that are white, yellow, pink or even red. They make wonderful hanging baskets of twiggy lacy stems.

R. mesembryanthoides has stiffish trailing stems up to a foot long, lined with ½-inch tubular joints that look like thick leaves. Pot in a mix of 1 part sphagnum moss, 1 part peat moss, 1 part perlite or sand. Keep moist in summer and rather dry in winter. You can leave them safely for a two- or three-week vacation at any time of year. Fertilize with a high nitrate formula and maintain temperatures over 65 degrees F. Place in Partial Sun. They are best grown in the window. We do not recommend them for the fluorescent light garden, although if you can find a place where they can trail, they do well under the artificial light. Propagate by stem cuttings that root easily in the same mix during the warm months. Plants are inexpensive and have many branches available for cutting material.

****

Rhipsalis are such a novelty to most people that they are a safe and satisfactory gift or benefit sales item. Many of the plants have widely spaced joints and tubular or square stems angling outward in intricate patterns. They will appeal both for their curious structure and their beauty when hung in the window.

We have become so fascinated with the different species of Rhipsalis that we are growing a large number in order to find out whether they are as suitable for indoor growing as they are good to look at. So far, our plants are confirming all our hopes. And we believe they can become among the most popular of indoor foliage plants. At present you will find a variety of species turning up in plant stores and garden centers. Grab them when you have the chance. They won't let you down.

CACTUS, RED BIRD. *Pedilanthus tithymaloides.*

Beginners
Party favors, benefits
Stem cuttings

Like many other plants commonly called Cactus, this one is nothing of the sort. It is a member of the Euphorbia family, which is not even distantly related to cactus. It is very popular out-of-doors in the southland where tall varieties are grown in clumps. Smaller kinds are of easiest culture in the house. It is definitely a beginner's plant.

Red Bird Cactus grows in clumps of upright unbranched stems, the leaves closely packed and opposite. They are 2 inches long, fleshy and more or less rectangular. When grown indoors, the variegated plants are preferred because the red flowers are rarely produced except under intense sun. Solid areas of white alternate with green on mature leaves, but new ones start out with touches of red.

Pot in sterilized garden soil with perlite added or in 1-1-1 soilless mix. Fertilize once a month during the summer with a balanced formula and keep moderately moist. Maintain a temperature over 65 degrees F. Grow under fluorescent light or in a sunny window. In winter, cut down on watering. The plant is essentially succulent and can go for a long period without moisture at that time. Propagation is by stem cuttings in the warm months. They root very easily in ordinary soil.

****

Small plants make excellent favors for parties and are perfect for the benefit table.

CACTUS, STAR. *Haworthia.*

Beginners
Gifts, housewarmings
Offsets

So many succulents that are not cacti are called Cactus that it is something of a scandal. Haworthia is not a difficult name to learn and, since it belongs to the lily family, it really has no resemblance to a cactus.

Haworthias are stemless or short-stemmed plants rarely more than a few inches high, with leaves arranged like a rose. There are a very great number of different species and the easiest of these are popular dish garden plants that any beginner can grow. That is because, unlike many succulents, they do not mind considerable watering and are not demanding of intense light. They can be grown in Partial Sun or 6 inches below

Planted in a pot or in feather rock, Star Cactus is an ideal small plant for a child or for a benefit sale.

the fluorescent tubes. Use 1-1-1 soilless mix with 2 tablespoons of lime chips added, water only when thoroughly dry, and maintain temperatures above 55 degrees F. They will survive lower temperatures but will then become sensitive to watering. Feed every couple of months with a high nitrate formula.

In summer, a healthy plant usually will be ringed by baby plants growing from beneath it. Once these have put down their own roots they can be separated and potted up. Subsequent growth is moderately rapid for a succulent. Occasionally, Haworthias are attacked by mealybug, which can be removed with a brush and rubbing alcohol.

****

There are two principal types of Haworthias. One has long, triangular, dark green leaves that are triangular also in cross-section. They grow out and upward, revealing their undersides, which have various arrangements of white raised pimples. *H. fasciata* and *margaritifera* are of this type. *H. reinwardtii* has the leaves arranged in a pillar and is taller than the others.

The other type has thicker, more rounded, softer leaves that are watery, often light green to bluish in color. The tips of the leaves are noticeably translucent. These plants, of which *H. cymbiformis* is typical, are more sensitive to watering and must be kept quite dry in winter. A good regimen is watering once a month from November through February, once every two weeks from March to June and September to November, and once a week in the summer months. They, too, produce offsets in considerable numbers.

They make nice gifts for small occasions and for benefits. If you happen to find a rare species—which is often no more difficult to grow than the common ones—you have a gift for an expert grower or specialist.

CALICO PLANT.
Alternanthera ficoidea (bettzickiana).
Beginners
Parties, benefits
Stem cuttings

Erect, stemmed plants with 3- to 5-inch leaves, narrowly to broadly spoon-shaped in many color variations. They can be grown by or given to a beginning indoor gardener. The requirements are temperatures over 60 degrees F., constant moisture and a balanced formula fertilizer. Pot in 2-1-1 soilless mix. Place in Partial Sun or close to fluorescent tubes. Propagation is from stem cuttings in soilless mix.

****

The Calico Plant has numerous variations with leaves orange and red in combination, pure yellow, or nearly pure red as in the variety 'Ruby'. Picking out a more attractively colored plant than average is important if you want to propagate it for friends.

The principal difficulty with *Alternanthera* is the matter of keeping it within bounds. It grows very rapidly and robustly so that it soon outgrows any pot you put it in. Stem after stem goes up and just keeps climbing until you have to nip it. If you have it under lights, you will find that it grows to the top of a shelf in a few weeks. You can then put it in the window where it will soon need a stake for support. If you cut it down, it looks unsightly.

This uncontrollable growth endears it to nurserymen, who can produce the plants from cuttings at great speed. And this same quality can be useful to you if you need lots of plants for parties or benefits. They make good sturdy foliage plants for the purpose but we must confess that, in spite of the descriptions, the colors are not luminous or bright and the general effect is not that enticing. Still, if a beginner wants to try a hand at propagation with a minimum of trouble, these are the plants for the purpose.

CHINESE EVERGREEN. *Aglaonema.*
Beginners
All major occasions
Stem cuttings

These are medium-size foliage plants with weak, fleshy stems and long, oval-pointed leaves, that can be grown by a beginner. Very little light is required; the plants do well in north light or under fluorescent lamps. They must be kept constantly moist and above 55 degrees F. Fertilize with a balanced formula. Grow in 3-2-1 soilless mix. Propagate by stem cuttings in moist vermiculite or water.

Aglaonemas in the market are mostly *A. commutatum*, but there are many forms. The leaves are 6 to 12 inches long and range from deep green with a few white spots to ones with as many as three shades of gray-green blotching in the spaces between the veins, making a herringbone pattern. In others, some of the blotches are yellowish. Thus, choosing a plant is a matter of taste.

****

There are very few problems in growing these plants. A peculiarity is that most of them do not look presentable until they have full-grown leaves. That means that they are not practical small gift plants. After reaching a height of 15 inches or so, when they look absolutely magnificent, the weak stems flop over and drape themselves over the sides of a pot or, if a long shallow container is provided, snake along the top of the soil. Indoors, some plants will produce insignificant flowers followed by oval red fruits that are ½-inch long and rather showy.

To multiply the plants, all you have to do is cut off stems and stick them in water. Keep them warm and in good light and they'll produce roots promptly.

As gifts, they are splendid if you develop them to the point where they have full-sized leaves. Three or four stems in a bonsai pot can be very handsome.

One species, *A. costatum*, is more compact. The leaves are black-green and covered with numerous brilliant white spots. It requires high humidity and should be grown in a terrarium. Since it produces offsets constantly, you can have plenty of plants of small size to put into gift terrariums. Because the leaves are closer together and the plant has a cusped appearance, it is more suitable than any other species for a compact, small gift of high quality, which will be appreciated by beginner and expert alike.

COCKSCOMB. *Celosia.*
Intermediates
Christmas, holidays
Stem cuttings

These are garden plants to be brought indoors in the fall. Since they will be past their prime and too large for the house, you should take cuttings and start new plants that will bloom again within a couple of months and be available for further cuttings or for gift giving as they are. Plants can also be started from seed in August or September for winter bloom.

They will grow best in sterilized garden soil with perlite added or in 1-1-1 soilless mix. Sand can be substituted for the perlite. Keep constantly moist as these are heavy drinkers, and give them deep pots to allow for a large root structure. Fertilize with a high phosphate-potash formula.

Celosia needs light every day and blooms better under fluorescent tubes than in the window. It is quite suitable for an intermediate grower. Cuttings root in 1-1-1 soilless mix without covering or in vermiculite.

****

Is it difficult for you to think of Cockscombs as blooming indoors? You are in for a surprise! The plants look far better in a pot than in the garden, where they seem stiff and ungainly. But choose dwarf plants, preferably of the pyramid or flame type. The wide, comb kind becomes somewhat disheveled. A yellow cockscomb in full bloom is one of the more spectacular house plants, and when it is in bloom from November to January or February, it brings summer back into the house.

Common as they are in the garden, they are appreciated by almost everyone as gifts in winter, and they are particularly suitable on holidays. The red and gold plants are right in the spirit of the Christmas season,

Many annuals can be grown from seed indoors in winter. Cockscomb looks better in the house than the garden and is a very acceptable gift.

and it is rather surprising that they are not sold at that time for their glorious plumes.

As long as you follow the simple directions, you will have no problem with these plants. They grow rapidly and uniformly into fully leaved and branched plants with a central plume and plenty of side ones. However, don't expect them to last forever and, as donor, don't give the impression that they will. Two or three months of bloom is all that can be expected. If further pleasure is to be derived from them, new cuttings must be started.

COLEUS. *Coleus blumei.*

Beginners, children
Party gifts, hostess presents
Stem cuttings, seed

Coleus are plants with multi-colored leaves growing to two feet high indoors. They grow in Bright Reflected light to Full Sun at over 60 degrees F. in sterilized garden soil with perlite added or in 1-1-1 soilless mix. Indoors, keep moderately moist in pots just big enough for the roots. Propagation is easy in soilless mix with stem cuttings or seed.

****

The great variety of foliage coloring makes a choice of a plant for propagation the most important item, if Coleus is to make an acceptable gift. Otherwise, the commonness of the plant handicaps it even for benefit sales. Plants can be brought in from the garden in the fall or started from seed at that time, and those with few but spectacular leaves are most desirable.

114

We recommend Coleus to beginners, for children, as modest party gifts and hostess presents. The best time to give them is in mid-winter when the plants are relatively scarce.

CORNSTALK PLANT. *Dracaena fragrans.* 'Massangeana'.

Beginners, children
Home decoration, housewarming gifts
Stem cuttings, offshoots

What we say for *Dracaena* also goes for the plants that are still called *Pleomele* in the shops but are now also listed as Dracaenas by botanists. Plants sometimes called Dracaenas are also to be found under *Cordyline* (Ti plants), the correct name. All of these plants have the same culture.

These are the toughest of house plants, tolerating temperatures down to 50 degrees F. and needing no more than north light. They can be potted in sterilized garden soil with perlite added, but will benefit from 3-2-1 soilless mix. Although preferring to be moderately moist, they can go for a week or two without any water. Even large plants can be grown in rather small containers. Propagation is by sections of stem laid on moist soil or sphagnum moss and kept warm in bright light. Some types produce many offshoots that can be potted up separately. When big canes have their tops cut off, branches will appear at the joints and these can be removed and grown. Often they will develop roots if placed in water. Fertilize occasionally with a high nitrate formula.

****

You can buy plants either as small juveniles for dish gardens or terrariums, or as thick canes with one or more new growths. The more attractive plants have the 12- to 24-inch long leaves striped vertically with ivory or white.

These are plants for rank beginners, for children, and for those who have little time or inclination to take care of them.

As big plants, they are useful for home decoration because they create large masses of foliage and are suitable for large pots or tubs. They are subject to mite and scale, but the leaves are easily cleaned.

The growing of sufficiently large and decorative Cornstalk Plants in home conditions takes more time and trouble than most people are willing to spend. Although the large plants make splendid gifts for most people, they are not a very practical choice. We include them here because they are so frequently grown. For the same reason, we want to mention the whole group of related plants with the same culture and a similar appearance.

D. deremensis 'Warneckii' is the familiar medium-sized plant with two white stripes running down the middle of the leaf. 'Janet Craig' is a recent compact introduction that looks best when about 2 feet high. *D. marginata* is the tall plant so often seen in banks and offices, with thin stems and narrow leaves at the top, dark green with a purple margin. *D. marginata* 'Tricolor' is a beautiful new form with the narrow leaves vertically striped in ivory, white and pink. If you can propagate this one you have a real winner, for it is one of the finest and showiest of modern plants. It looks best when about 2 feet high, as its colors are best seen from above. *D. surculosa* (godseffiana) is quite a different plant, for it is woody and branched, grows usually no more than a foot and a half high indoors and has 3-inch oval leaves spotted with white or yellow.

Closely related and with the same culture is the Ti plant, *Cordyline terminalis.* This is similar to the Cornstalk Plant in growth but with shorter leaves. Some of the varieties have reddish-margined leaves, especially the brilliant variety 'Baby Doll'. *Cordyline indivisa*, the Blue Dracaena, has green leaves with a bluish cast.

CRAPE MYRTLETTE. *Lagerstroemia indica.*
Intermediates, experts
Party gifts and favors, benefits, birthdays
Seed, cuttings

These are small flowering shrubs for intermediate and expert growers that can also be bloomed in the summer garden. Seed planted in finely sieved packaged or homemade soilless mix germinates promptly. When plants are a couple of inches high, they will start to bloom. Remove all buds until they gain strength and keep trimming lead leaves to produce branches.

For growth and bloom, the plants should be kept at over 60 degrees F. Seedlings can be transplanted to pots with 2-1-1 soilless mix. Feed with a high nitrate fertilizer in the early stages but switch to high phosphate-potash when the plants are large enough to bloom properly. Maintain plants moist at all times. Keep in Partial or Full Sun or 3 inches below the fluorescent lamps. You can also multiply by means of cuttings of partly mature wood in peat moss or Jiffy 7's.

****

The Crape Myrtlette is a miniature edition of the well-known garden shrub Crape Myrtle that grows throughout the South. They are of comparatively recent introduction and are among our most attractive house plants. Flowers consisting of very ruffled petals come in white, pink and red and are 1 to 1½ inches across, produced throughout the year. However, the plant becomes woody after about a year, and more seeds must be planted or cuttings rooted.

These superb plants make cherished gifts in any size. Even those who cannot take care of them properly can enjoy their flowers for a while. All the recipient has to do is water them. Four-inch plants in 2-inch pots make splendid party gifts and will sell fast on the benefit sale table. Give larger plants for more important occasions. These are plants that are worthy of good-looking pots.

CROSSANDRA. *Crossandra infundibuliformis.*
Intermediates, experts, specialist-hobbyists
Holiday gifts, parties, sales
Stem cuttings, seed

These handsome flowering plants with their fan-shaped orange blossoms that are produced over a long period are among the easiest to multiply. Most seedsmen carry them, but germination is very slow so that it is both easier and more rapid to buy a plant and make cuttings which root promptly in soilless mix. The plants are generally available in the shops in the spring, but flowering can be continued around the year.

We recommend these to intermediate and expert growers rather than beginners only because they do require regular attention. They grow best in 2-1-1 soilless mix with lime added, kept moist at 65 degrees F. or higher, and fertilized with a high phosphate-potash formula. Plants from cuttings should be nipped to cause them to branch. About a month is required between rooting of the stem cutting and setting of the first buds. Keep the plants within 6 inches of the fluorescent tubes or in a sunny window. They are not likely to bloom in daylight in winter.

****

Like so many other attractive blooming plants, Crossandras have a relatively short blooming life—about 9 months. For winter flowering, cuttings should be rooted in September or early October; root again in late December for spring giving. Indoors, growth is not as luxuriant as in a greenhouse. For larger gift plants, it is therefore advisable to have two cuttings in a 4-inch azalea pot or four cuttings in a 6-incher. Fertilize heavily and keep constantly moist.

Crossandras are subject to mite and occasionally to mealybug but are not excessively leafy and can be cleaned up rather easily.

Because of their bright-green 4-inch leaves and brilliant flowering, Crossandras are valued by amateurs or experts. They are not common in stores and, especially in winter, they are one of the very best gift choices.

Single plants are fine—and will bloom—in 2-inch pots for parties and sales. Larger plants will please a hostess or be an adornment and gift for a holiday. Even the specialist-hobbyist will appreciate a plant as a gift.

The ease with which Crossandra can be multiplied from cuttings makes it one of our most useful gift plants. Once you have a plant, you can start others and allow them to grow large so that you always have cutting material for a planned gift.

DWARF CROWN OF THORNS. *Euphorbia millii.* 'Bojeri'.

Intermediates
Birthdays, anniversaries, all occasions
Stem cuttings

The dwarf Crown of Thorns is quite easy for an intermediate grower. The only important trick is to keep it constantly wet, contrary to the advice given in so many books. Only if this treatment is followed will the plant remain constantly in leaf and produce flowers throughout the year. It does require Partial or Full Sun and therefore cannot be bloomed in winter except under fluorescent light. It should be placed with the top no more than 3 inches below the tubes.

Pot in 2-1-1 soilless mix and fertilize with a balanced formula. The plant is a heavy drinker and consumer of fertilizer. It grows quickly, too, requiring frequent trimming which will make it branch. Maintain the temperature above 65 degrees F. at all times.

Seed is not available, but cuttings of plants bought in the market will root if taken during an active growing period between summer and fall. When the stem is cut, it bleeds a white fluid. Dry up this liquid on the cutting with a match or cigarette lighter without severely burning the cut end. Then plant in dry vermiculite and spray daily until it starts to grow. Place in the best light and the warmest place you have. Over-watering will cause the cutting to rot.

****

The flowers of Crown of Thorns consist of two colored leaves like petals. They are small, but the bright, brick-red is very showy against the light green, spoon-shaped leaves. Hybrids with larger white or yellow flowers are more difficult to grow and do not do well indoors. The small variety 'Bojeri' is the easiest and most floriferous. A still more dwarf type often turns up in variety stores. The little bushes are thorny and should be handled with care.

Trim these plants and use the cuttings for propagation. With careful pruning the plant becomes a small tree that can be spectacular in a deep bonsai pot. They are fine plants for favors and benefit sales when small. Large plants are respectable gifts for birthdays, anniversaries and other special occasions. They are easily bloomed in winter and their color is appropriate both to the Christmas season and to spring holidays.

DAHLBORG DAISY. *Thymophylla.*

Inexperienced growers
Fund raising sales, party favors, children
Seed

This little plant produces 1-inch yellow daisies in profusion and is one of the easiest annuals to grow indoors. It makes a charming little gift plant.

Use five seeds to a 4-inch pot of moist 1-1-1 soilless mix. Plant just below the surface and sprinkle lightly with milled sphagnum moss to prevent damp-off, a fungus infection of seedlings. Put the four seeds around the sides and one seed in the middle. If any of the seeds do not come up after a week, reseed.

As soon as green shows, place the pot with the top within 3 inches of the fluorescent lamps and keep it there throughout the subsequent growth. The plants are delicate-stemmed and tend to trail. Leaves are feathery. Nip the tips as soon as you have six leaves so that they will branch. Don't worry if the stems fall over. Just rearrange them so that they look well in the pot. Flowering should start within a month and continue for eight weeks or more. Keep just moist and fertilize with a balanced formula. Remove the remains of flowers, each of which lasts a few days.

****

These little plants make excellent gifts for inexperienced growers and for fund raising sales. But they should only be attempted from seed if you have a very sunny window or fluorescent lights. Cuttings will root but are not advisable. A packet of seeds will take care of all your needs.

DRUNKARD'S DREAM. *Hatiora salicornioides.*

Beginners, young people
Hostess gifts, housewarmings
Stem cuttings

Drunkard's Dream is a trailing, somewhat shrubby plant without leaves, that makes an excellent show in a small basket. It should be potted indoors in a mix of 1 part sphagnum moss, 1 part peat moss, 1 part perlite and 1 part vermiculite. Hang in Bright Reflected light where the temperature will always be above 60 degrees F. Keep constantly moist in summer and rather dry in winter. This is a good vacation plant at that time. Fertilize sparingly with fish emulsion. Cuttings root in Jiffy 7's or sphagnum moss kept moist.

****

The stems of *Hatiora* become quite woody with time, but the many branches consist of what appear to be little bottles ½ inch long, strung on green wires—hence the name. The effect is very airy and lacy. This is a sturdy plant that even a beginner can handle once it has been properly potted.

As a gift, its merit is in its oddity and graceful habit. It is a bit too plain-looking to be attractive for buyers at benefit sales. But when a plant has been grown on for a while and has developed several branches, it is a fine gift in a 4-inch pot for a hostess, for young people, or for a housewarming. With little care it can grow into an imposing specimen. The plant is very nearly disease-free and care-free as well.

EARTH STARS. *Cryptanthus.*

Intermediates, experts
Gift for ill or hospitalized
Offsets

These are small bromeliads with very short stems and overlapping long, narrow leaves that lie flat so that the whole plant is rarely more than 3 inches high. The leaves are very dry and hard but beautifully patterned with horizontal or vertical stripes in rich colors.

The plants will only keep their flat form and good color if they have plenty of light. This means they need to be kept in a sunny windowsill in summer and close to artificial light in winter. Soil is quite unimportant as long as it has good drainage. You can use soilless mix, sphagnum moss or a mixture of the mix and the moss. Garden soil (sterilized) bakes too hard but is suitable with one third perlite added. The plants should be moistened weekly in summer and once every two weeks in winter. They benefit from daily misting. Fertilize with a high nitrate formula no more than once a month.

Propagation is by detaching and planting offsets that grow out from under the plant in considerable numbers.

We consider *Cryptanthus,* in spite of its apparent ease of culture, at least an intermediate plant.

****

We should like to note first of all that we do not recommend most other bromeliads because, if showy, they are too big and difficult to grow well. The big plants with startling flower stalks that are seen in the flower shops last very well but, like all bromeliads, they die after bloom is over. The plants continue living on by means of offsets that appear at this time. But only experts can grow these pups to maturity and cause them to bloom again.

In the case of *Cryptanthus*, the bloom is not important and the plants are small. The yield of offsets is often between five and 10 per plant, and each of these will develop nicely without too much trouble.

The vertically striped plants are mostly *C. acaulis*. In these the stripes are combinations of ivory, brown, green and bright pink—as showy as any flower. The horizontally-striped plants are *C. zonatus*. The leaves are longer—up to 9 inches—and the alternating stripes are mostly gray and brown.

Earth Stars make beautiful and desirable gifts for special occasions. Since the yield of plants is not large, they should be grown on to look their best and potted in the handsomest manner possible. We recommend them as gifts for almost any major occasion, for well-grown plants are not common and even an expert will appreciate a fine-colored specimen. We suggest it also as a plant for an ill person because it will go without water for weeks and, with only a minimum degree of attention, will last a year. Meanwhile, its rich coloring will bring cheer.

Incidentally, Earth Stars are quite inexpensive by mail order.

ELFIN HERB. *Cuphea hyssopifolia.*
Intermediates
Party favors, benefits, important gifts
Stem cuttings

Elfin Herb is an easy little shrub growing no more than a foot high and producing numerous pink-violet flowers no more than ⅜-inch across. It is an ideal plant for the intermediate grower.

Plant in 3-2-1 soilless mix and keep moist at all times For bloom it requires Partial Sun or a position 4 to 6 inches under the lights. It also needs continuous moisture. Fertilize with a balanced formula. Propagation is by stem cuttings.

****

Seed can be bought, but we recommend buying a good-sized mature plant with many branches. Seed can be collected by shaking the branches over a sheet of paper a few weeks after the start of bloom. Germination is easy, but growth to flowering size will take time. Since the plant branches naturally, there is plenty of cutting material and the yield is much quicker. Cuttings should be rooted in vermiculite in a closed propagation box, and will soon start blooming. Maintain temperature above 65 degrees F.

Older plants are very handsome and can be trimmed to a nearly bonsai appearance. The less-than-one-inch-long narrow leaves contribute to the effect of a heather-like miniature of a large shrub.

Since small flowers look larger on small plants, Elfin Herb in a 2-inch pot makes a respectable and unusual party favor or a plant for the benefit sale table, while larger plants in artistic pots are altogether charming and worthy of important gift giving.

Defoliation through mite attacks does occur with these plants, but the pests are easy to control by subjecting the plant to frequent washings.

EPISCIA.

Intermediates, experts
Party gifts, benefits, big occasions
Stem cuttings

Episcias are colorful foliage plants for pots and baskets. In addition, some can be kept in bloom all year long if the temperature remains over 65 degrees F. and the humidity not under 30 percent. This makes them plants for intermediate or expert growers rather than the beginner. They require potting in 2-1-1 soilless mix with 2 tablespoons of lime chips or crushed eggshell added to the quart. Fertilize with a high phosphate-potash formula and fish emulsion. If only leaves are desired, plants can be kept in Bright Reflected light or at the end of the fluorescent tubes. Flowering requires Partial Sun and a more central position under the lights. The plants should be kept moist, but are sensitive to overwatering. Thus, some drying out between waterings is advisable. Propagation is by stem cuttings and tips of stolons.

****

The stems of Episcias are thick and trailing. The leaves are 3 to 6 inches long, oval and heavily veined. There are two basic types: those with hairy, velvety surfaces in apple-green, and those with relatively smooth surfaces that are quilted and combine zones of brown and silver. They have been so much hybridized that the range of coloring has been extended to a remarkable degree. Leaves can be so beautiful as to be worth growing for themselves alone. There are plants that bloom easily and others that are unreliable.

The flowers are only an inch across, consisting of a tube and a more-or-less flat, flared, five-lobed face. The colors are mostly brilliant tomato-red to pink. There are also yellow-, white- and blue-purple-flowered types, but we cannot recommend these, either because of growing diffi-

122

culty or because they have relatively unattractive flowers and leaves. Our favorite plants are 'Moss Agate', with large green leaves veined with silver; 'Silver Sheen' and 'Shimmer', the leaves zoned in metallic silver and brown; 'Chocolate Soldier', with brown leaves; and 'Colombian Orange' with small, plush, green leaves. A famous plant, 'Cleopatra', having large leaves zoned in white, green and pink, can be grown without much difficulty in a terrarium.

The main stem of an Episcia is a thick, juicy one that needs a small stake when only a few inches high. Many stolons—rope-like branches without joints—grow from the stem. At the ends of these appear clusters of leaves and sometimes flowers. When the tip of a stolon is pinned down in a pot (soil layered), it will root, and the connection with the parent can then be severed. Pieces of stem with leaf also root easily in vermiculite in a closed container as long as the moisture content of the mix is very low. Once the plants are rooted, growth is quite rapid. Bloom may start on quite small plants.

Well-grown Episcia plantlets in 2-inch pots are very attractive gifts for parties and for sale at benefits. Larger plants make a magnificent show either in azalea pots or hanging baskets and make luxury gifts for the big occasions.

EXACUM AFFINE.
Intermediates, experts
Party favors, benefits, hostess gift
Seed

Exacums grow, at most, to a foot high and across. They have fleshy stems and bright green, 1-inch long, fleshy leaves with very short stalks. This plant is grown for its flowers, which are about ½ inch across, quite blue, and five-petalled, with a cluster of yellow stamens projecting from the center.

They are grown only from seed, which is readily available and germinates promptly in sieved soilless mix. Grow in 2-1-1 mix and keep moist at all times. Fertilize with a high phosphate-potash formula. Place in Partial Sun or within 4 inches of the fluorescent tubes. Remove the many dead flowers. Maintain the temperature above 65 degrees F.

****

Exacums can be grown outdoors in summer and brought indoors in the fall. But is is better to start with young plants for the winter season when they are most desirable. Seeded in September, you can have them blooming right through the cold weather. However, you will find it difficult to keep them blooming in the window. Artificial lighting results are much better.

A naturally branching plant, it needs no trimming. But the removal of old flowers is mandatory since it produces them in great numbers. Figure on your plant lasting no more than nine months.

A flowering plant is a fine gift for an intermediate or expert grower. Young plants just starting to bloom make splendid subjects for party favors and will go like hot cakes on the benefit sale table. It does not make a big or lasting gift for a major occasion.

FERN, BOSTON, FINE-LEAVED. *Nephrolepis.*
'Whitmanii' and 'Norwoodii'.
Intermediates, experts
Any occasion
Division

For the intermediate and expert grower, these are plants that should always be in the indoor garden. They have the most delicate of leaves, the leaflets so divided as to appear to consist of several layers. Plants are a foot high in a 6-inch azalea pot and about 15 inches across. Pot in 3-2-1 soilless mix and keep constantly moist, fertilizing regularly with fish emulsion. They can be grown in an east window or in Bright Reflected light and 6 inches below the fluorescent tubes.

These ferns increase by means of thread-like stolons that root at the tips. Thus, each plant consists of a number of tufts, and when these have spread sufficiently and are numerous, they can be cut apart with soil adhering and potted up separately. Keep the temperature above 65 degrees F. at all times.

****

These wonderful ferns are far easier to grow than their appearance suggests. They look so tropical that you would guess that only greenhouse conditions could suffice. However, we have grown them for years in a living room that, in winter, is consistently low in humidity. One plant, bought 15 or more years ago, has yielded hundreds of young plants and is still going strong.

The one thing they do need is good grooming. Old leaves should be cut off and sometimes the tufts in the center of a pot dry up and must be removed. Separated plants grow rapidly into fine specimens.

Far superior to 'Fluffy Ruffles' and the Compact Boston Fern, they make first-class gifts for any occasion.

Whether you are giving 2-inch pot plants at parties, or selling them at benefits, or presenting a big potted one as a gift for a holiday, a housewarming or even a birthday, these plants will always arouse wonder and incur gratitude. Larger plants should go to people who can treat them to their minimum requirements. Careful instructions will help.

Of the two plants, we prefer *N.* 'Norwoodii', which is a bit more difficult to come by in the shops.

FERN, MAIDENHAIR. *Adiantum.*
Experts, specialist-hobbyists
Housewarming, hostess gifts
Division

The Maidenhair Ferns are very tempting because of their airy beauty but are not recommended except for expert growers. They will grow in low light but require very high humidity and coolness. They do not do well in a terrarium. They are acceptable presents for fern hobbyists.

FERN, RABBIT'S FOOT. *Davallia fejeensis.*
Intermediates, experts
Any important occasion
Leaf cuttings

This is one of the several basket ferns with coarse wooly rhizomes that curve over the sides of a container. They are not difficult plants, but we would rate them intermediate to expert because of the constant watching that is required.

They do well in a 3-2-1 soilless mix or in a mix made with sphagnum moss, some peat moss and some perlite—the last two to give a little firmness to the medium. The fern is shallow-rooted and must be kept constantly moist. Maintain temperature above 65 degrees F. High humidity improves performance but is not a necessity. Fertilize with a high nitrate formula. Hang in Bright Reflected or Partial Sun.

Propagation is by cutting sections of rhizome with a leaf or two and pressing horizontally into the soilless mix. Keep spraying daily until rooted.

****

These ferns are subject to scale. If attacked, cut off all the leaves down to the rhizomes and wash the latter off thoroughly with rubbing alcohol and a stiff brush. Or, put the pot into a plastic bag with a section of No-Pest Strip overnight.

As gifts, small-rooted plants are treasured and a basket is worthy of an important occasion.

FIG, CREEPING. *Ficus pumila.*

Intermediates
Gift terrariums for the ill, young people, all occasions
Stem cuttings

This is a creeping, trailing, small-leaved plant that clings to walls or glass. It is strictly a terrarium plant for an intermediate grower. It requires a minimum of 65 degrees F., 2-1-1 soilless mix and occasional fertilizing with a balanced formula. A north window or 2 feet below the fluorescent tubes is sufficient. Propagation is by stem cuttings in a terrarium or closed propagation box.

We list none of the large figs, although there are many that are fine, large ornamentals. They are capable of being air-layered, and seed of some of them is available from mail-order houses. But we consider the process too slow, and presentable plants are expected to be too large. The plants have not been expensive in the shops.

The Mistletoe Fig, *Ficus deltoidea (diversifolia)*, is a shrub for expert growers, growing a maximum of 12 inches indoors and bearing little green fruits. It can be propagated from stem cuttings and makes an excellent gift plant, though slow growing.

But for general use and gift giving, the miniature trailing (or climbing) figs are ideal. Most of them have green, oval, pointed leaves ranging in size from ½ to 1½ inches. They grow beautifully in a terrarium of any size, creeping up the walls by adhesive roots and covering them with a network of greenery. Our favorite is the form *quercifolia*, the Oak Leaf Miniature Fig. The little leaves are roughly shield-shaped, lobed and quilted—a more interesting leaf design than the normal plants.

These figs only require typical terrarium conditions (see Chapter 5). Pieces of stem root quickly if planted in the terrarium itself and soon grow to a point where they are presentable.

Grown in small terrariums and reaching up to 10 inches in diameter, they are ideal as gifts for the ill, for young people and as hostess presents because they need no attention whatsoever for long periods of time. Small terrariums—tiny glass snifters, for instance—are fine for shower and party guests, and for benefit sales.

For larger, more important presents, these figs are used as part of a planting. For instance, combined with broader-leaved, more colorful foliage plants, they can be placed along the wall of a rectangular terrarium to make an attractive foliage background for the planting.

Mistletoe Fig (*Ficus diversifolia*), an ideal gift shrub.

FITTONIA. Mosaic Plant. Silver Nerve Plant.
Beginners, intermediates
Terrariums for children, anniversary gifts
Stem cuttings

Fittonias are colorful and easy foliage plants for a pot or small basket. We rate them beginner to intermediate in culture which is the same as for most of these tropical plants. They require Partial Sun or Bright Reflected light or a position about 12 inches under the fluorescent tubes. Keep moist at all times and over 65 degrees F. Fertilize with a balanced formula, using 2-1-1 soilless mix. Propagation is by stem cuttings.

* * * * * * * * * * * * * * * *

Fittonia is a sprawler with oval leaves up to 6 inches long. There are two types of coloration. In one, the very fine network of veins is red or carmine; in the other, they are white. Both kinds are equally attractive. Recently the white-veined Fittonia has been bred in various sized leaves down to a plant with 1-inchers, called Fittonia 'Minima'. This little plant has become popular in a very short time, being neat and crisp-looking and ideal for 2- or 3-inch pot culture or a small terrarium.

Because Fittonias can be grown either small or quite large and impressively showy, they are good gifts for most occasions. The small white-nerved type is fine for sales, for favors and small hostess presents. The larger plants will please even the exotic grower if several stems are grown in a 6-inch pot.

GERANIUM, ROSE or SCENTED. *Pelargonium.*
Experts
Party and shower favors, benefits, housewarmings
Stem cuttings

The various species of scented geraniums have small but sometimes pretty flowers. However, they are grown preferably as foliage plants and are cherished for their various rose, lemon and other fruity or aromatic odors.

Keeping the plants alive is not difficult, but growing good-looking ones is. So we believe that they need the care of a fairly experienced grower, although the details of culture are simple enough.

Indoors, use a mix consisting of 4 parts ordinary packaged potting soil, ½ part vermiculite, ½ part perlite and ½ part small-grained bird gravel. Fertilize with a balanced formula once a week in summer, once a month in winter. Unlike many geraniums, these generally require regular moisture—a couple of days without watering and they droop. Most of them become lanky in growth no matter how much sun we give them indoors or how close we put them to the lights. They look best, in fact, as young, half-grown plants from cuttings. However, it must be said that even when rather tall, some of the finer-leaved plants look well if supported by a stake. The lemon geraniums of the *P. crispum* kinds are more compact and must be watered more carefully as they dry out easily, yet rot easily if over-watered.

Propagate by taking stem cuttings and planting in the same potting mix. Placed under bright light and misted daily—not watered—they do put out roots, begin to grow and can then be watered regularly. Plants that bloom in summer, such as the Oak Leaf Geranium, are fed a high phosphate-potash fertilizer at that time.

****

As small plants in small pots, these delicious-smelling plants are more appreciated as gifts for parties, shower favors and sale tables, especially in winter, than for more important occasions.

A word must be said about other types of geraniums. Contrary to the hopes of many, the large-flowered geraniums do not do well enough indoors to grow into compact plants or to bloom as they do outdoors. Miniature geraniums are delightful and make perfect gifts for any occasion, but require cool conditions. They grow best in the 55- to 65-degree F. range, within 3 inches of fluorescent lamps. They must be allowed to dry out well between waterings. They will survive for a while on a shelf at ordinary house temperatures, but will eventually succumb to fungal diseases. If you have the means to grow these plants at the requisite temperatures, you'll have an ideal plant for giving. Air conditioning does help and solves the problem with some of these plants. 'Variegated Prince Rupert', a shy bloomer but a lovely foliage plant, does better than most and can be trained into bonsai form or on a ring. But we must warn that unless the recipient of these plants has the proper conditions, the pleasure of the gift will be short-lived.

On the whole, it is advisable to stick to the scented geraniums. And, if you find a plant that grows well for you, hang on to it, multiply it and depend on it for your stock of geranium gifts.

The Goldfish Plant (*Columnea*) makes superb flowering basket presents for intermediate and expert growers.

GOLDFISH PLANT. *Columnea.*

Intermediates, experts
Important presents, housewarmings
Stem cuttings, seed

Columneas are mostly trailing basket plants with a few having a more upright habit. Their flowers are extraordinary 1½- to 3½-inch tubes, brilliant yellow, orange or red, with long projecting upper lips and side wings that make them look rather fish-like. In a greenhouse or sun porch the stems can trail as much as 6 feet, and the floriferousness is tremendous. We would rate this the most showy basket plant now in cultivation.

There are plants with seasonal bloom and a few that can be counted on throughout the year as long as the environment is favorable. They do require good intermediate to expert handling, which is the reason why we rarely see them in the shops but why they are quite common in the collections of good amateur indoor growers.

Use 2-1-1 soilless mix with 2 tablespoons of lime chips or crushed eggshell to the quart. Columneas don't want to be totally dry at any time, but soaking is dangerous to them, especially when the temperature drops. What is required is a combination of humidity over 60 percent and temperature over 65 degrees F. at all times, with the soil well aerated but never soggy. Fertilize with a high phosphate-potash formula.

The light requirement is Partial to Full Sun or about 400 foot-candles under fluorescent tubes. Plants of different kinds vary in their needs. Propagation is by stem cuttings in vermiculite with covering and warmth. Seed is also available, but most of the hybrids are sterile.

****

Columneas have been widely hybridized, but there is only one that we can recommend strongly as being compact enough so that it can be grown either in a basket or under fluorescent light, where it does best. And it is the only one we know that is relatively easy to bloom indoors and is truly everblooming with some care. This is *C.* 'Chanticleer', which has orange 1½-inch flowers. It is neither the most prolific nor the showiest of Goldfish plants but, when well-grown, is sturdy and handsome. It is one of the few plants that submits to trimming and training.

A big basket of such a magnificent plant is the finest of gifts for anyone who can take care of it and has the space. The good varieties can only be bought from gesneriad specialist nurseries. And growing large and handsome plants is a difficult matter in the house. 'Chanticleer' is about the only one that yields reliable results and can be gifted either as a small blooming cutting or a medium-size basket plant or pot. Being rather rigid, it rarely grows bigger than a foot across, branches more than most, and looks neat at all times.

GRAPE IVY. *Cissus rhombifolia.*
Kangaroo Vine. *Cissus antartica.*
Beginners
Housewarmings, shower presents, children
Stem cuttings

Both of these vines are popular cast iron plants with tendrils, usually grown in baskets and much alike in appearance. They prefer 3-2-1 soilless mix, a high nitrate fertilizer and moderate watering. They can be grown in Light Shade in a north window or under less than 100 footcandles of fluorescent or Wonderlite lamp. Temperature should be over 50 degrees F. Fast growers, they need trimming when branches become too long. Propagation is by stem cuttings. They are definitely beginners' plants.

****

The Kangaroo Vine is the coarser and faster-growing of the two, with simple, oblong, leathery, toothed leaves 3 to 4 inches long. Leaves are rather widely spaced, but there is plenty of branching.

Grape Ivy is more graceful, and has leaves consisting of three leaflets that are coarsely lobed. Recently improved varieties, including one called 'Ellen Danica', have somewhat prettier foliage.

These plants are useful as greenery in public places and in homes where a mass of foliage is more important than elegance. Although preferring regular watering, they can go for a week or so without moisture, showing no ill effects.

We can recommend them as gifts only if grown to large basket plant proportions. This can be done in a few months by planting a number of cuttings in a basket, supplying warmth and more than the minimum light requirements, and fertilizing with every watering.

IMPATIENS. Busy Lizzy.
All growers
Favors, benefits, especially in winter
Stem cuttings, seed

The culture and propagation of Impatiens indoors is the same as for Balsam except that its light requirements are lower. It can also be brought in from the garden, and dwarf plants are by far the best. The same conditions control seeding and the rooting of stem cuttings. As for light, Partial Sun and 6 to 10 inches under the tubes will suffice. But Impatiens is more rewarding than Balsam, produces more compact plants and has a greater variety of coloring. Since it is a perennial, you can expect a longer season with these plants.

Impatiens does well in Partial Sun and under fluorescent lighting, though some varieties grow too tall for shelf culture. Pot in sterilized garden soil with perlite in a proportion of 5 to 1. As bloom is not important, fertilize with a high nitrate formula. The temperature should not go below 60 degrees F. Water after the surface of the soil has dried out.

****

Our remarks about Balsams as gifts need not be repeated here for Impatiens. The problem is obviously the same, and winter is the time to give. Choosing a colorful and compact plant to multiply is important. If you start from seed, figure three months to flowering.

Some of the newly-introduced New Guinea varieties are very beautiful. But thus far, they have proved cool growers and are subject to fungal attacks. If you find a plant with really colorful leaves, it might be worth growing for these alone. But our experience is that the variegated New Guinea plants do as poorly as the blooming types.

IVY. *Hedera helix.*
Experts, specialist-hobbyists
Table favors, hospitality gifts
Stem cuttings

Although not really good house plants, and although many of the finest small varieties grow painfully slowly, ivies are good gift plants because they are popular. Some plants are considered very choice. The difficulties are due to the need for quite cool conditions and their receptivity to pests, especially mites.

Ivies will grow faster in a rich soil but, unfortunately, most of the variegated ones tend to revert to green if pampered. So the best soil is probably from the garden, sterilized, of course, and mixed with a little perlite to improve drainage. Most ivies should be kept moist at all times for good growth, but some of the choice miniatures will begin to look like ordinary plants unless kept rather dry. Fertilize not more than once a month with a balanced formula. A temperature of 50 to 75 degrees F. is best.

Light requirement is quite low. In fact, the plants will grow more slowly in Partial Sun than in Light Shade.

Propagate by stem cuttings in a mixture of half and half perlite and vermiculite.

****

From the above description, it is apparent that ivies are variable and that plants react differently to treatment. In addition to mites, they get every other known infestation. The fine variegated plants are temperamental, and the tiny-leaved plants that are popular for dish gardens and terrariums grow so slowly that propagating requires maximum patience.

For gifting, the first requirement is finding an unusual-looking or rare plant. We can't advise you on this as it is purely a matter of taste.

One form of ivy-growing that has become something of a craze and that certainly results in a rather impressive gift is artificial topiary. Real topiary results from long and patient trimming of plants. The artificial kind involves stuffing wire forms of animals or other shapes with moist sphagnum moss and then pinning cuttings into it with hairpins. By keeping the form moist, giving it moderate light and fussing over it a bit, you can soon have a decorative product. In fact, if you have enough cuttings, you can produce the results in a few hours. Topiary forms can be bought ready-made for hobbyist ivy growers.

These temporary plantings must be kept cool and constantly moist once the cuttings have rooted. Sections that die out can be replaced with new cuttings. All in all, this is a most showy gift for anybody who has a taste for such things.

IVY, SWEDISH. *Plectranthus oertendahlii.*

Beginners
Home decoration, any occasion
Stem cuttings

Swedish Ivy is a trailing basket plant for a beginner. The stems are fleshy and lax, the leaves medium green, somewhat kidney-shaped, 1½ inches across, and shallowly lobed. The edges turn down, giving a cupped effect.

Grow in 2-1-1 soilless mix, keep moist at all times, and feed with a high nitrate fertilizer. North light is sufficient. Propagation is easy in soilless mix by means of stem cuttings.

****

A large basket of Swedish Ivy may be an acceptable gift for decorating a home. But for most purposes the plant is too common. There is, however, a way of turning it into a more desirable present. The roots are shallow and, if planted in a clay saucer that is an inch or more deep, it will spread beautifully in a couple of months and be a prettier plant than you could have believed possible. When grown under fluorescent light at a distance of no more than 6 inches, it will produce spires of small violet flowers. In this state it makes a charming present for any type of grower and almost any occasion. The one factor that must be watched by both grower and recipient is the moisture. In such a shallow container, water evaporates rather quickly, so moisture must be maintained at all times. A daily light watering is almost always necessary.

JADE TREE. *Crassula argentea.*

All growers
Hostess presents, hospital gift
Stem and leaf cuttings

Jade trees have thick rubbery trunks and teardrop-shaped, thick green leaves often edged with red. There are varieties with large or small leaves. We prefer the large-leaved kind that develop after a few years into superb pot specimens up to 3 feet high and as much across. With judicious pruning the branches become more prominent and thicker,

A fine specimen such as this *Crassula argentea* in a classic pot is a major gift for any occasion, yet is easy to grow.

giving them a powerful sculptural look.

They are succulents that need potting in 1-1-1 soilless mix and are to be kept moderately moist during the summer months. In winter, water once a week. The amount of water depends on the size of the plant and whether or not there is much sun. Give less moisture than is required to soak the pot completely. Leaves can shrivel both from over- and under-watering, but the latter does less damage. To avoid growing long branches with few leaves, keep in Partial or Full Sun, not under artificial light. Fertilize with a high nitrate formula no more than three or four times during the summer.

Although the Jade plant grows quite slowly, it does branch freely, providing numerous cuttings. Sections of stem and leaf root easily in the same soilless mix when very moderately watered and kept warm and in the sun.

****

As gift plants, Jade trees suffer from being so common. But if you train small plants carefully so that they have a good shape, they make pleasant hostess presents. A mature plant in a large decorative pot can be an important present that is relatively carefree.

Lantana is a suprisingly easy plant to flower indoors and can also be grown as a little tree. This one is no more than a year old.

DWARF LANTANA. *Lantana nana compacta.*
Intermediates, experts
All occasions, in winter
Stem cuttings, seed

The dwarf Lantana is far less common than the larger basket types of plants but it is the only one suitable for growing indoors. You will be surprised at the neatness of these plants, the ease with which they bloom and the large size and bright coloring of the flowers.

Grow in 2-1-1 soilless mix with two tablespoons of lime chips or crushed eggshell to the quart. Keep constantly moist. Fertilize frequently with a high nitrate formula. Maintain the temperature over 60 degrees F. Place the plants with their tops within 4 inches of the fluorescent tubes or set in Full Sun. They are best suited for intermediate to expert growers. Propagation is by seed or stem cuttings.

****

136

Although seldom grown indoors, the dwarf Lantana is one of the half dozen best blooming plants for the house. It is well known that it attracts white flies. If you bring these plants in from the garden, spray with House and Garden Raid on the undersides of the leaves every two days until all signs of the insects have disappeared. Indoor-grown plants can be kept clean if you watch them and take action at the first sign of infestation.

A peculiarity of Lantana is its thirst. It looks like a dry plant, but slurps up water from the soil at a fantastic rate. It doesn't want to be soggy for long, but don't let it dry out completely, either.

The plant is a fast grower and blooms quickly from cuttings. Seed is variable—one may come up in a month, others may stay dormant for a year or more. You would be wise to buy a plant at a nursery in late spring as you will then have the means to make as many plants as you wish. Our own Lantanas all come from two plants bought at least 10 years ago. The parents have long since died, but the progeny go on and on.

Grow the cuttings in slightly moistened vermiculite without covering. Since branches develop quickly on the plants, there is always plenty of cutting material handy.

Lantanas become woody with age but increase in beauty. Within less than nine months you can have a little tree with short woody branches and new green growths bearing the flowers in profusion. These make splendid gifts and require less training to produce beautiful results than any other plant we know. Thus, Lantana can be a surprising and welcome gift. However, as with all the summer flowering plants, we suggest gifting for all purposes in winter.

LAVENDER. *Lavandula dentata.* French Lavender.
Intermediates, experts
Favors, hospitality gifts, benefits
Seed, cuttings

This is a very fine-leaved Lavender that adapts far better to indoor growing than the English plants and is much more perfumed. Seed takes about two weeks to germinate and cuttings do not root very easily. Cuttings should be grown in vermiculite or peat pellets and kept just moist. Do not cover the cuttings but keep between 75 and 80 degrees F.

Once the plants are rooted or the seeds are well germinated, culture is easier. Grow in 2-1-1 soilless mix with 2 tablespoons of powdered lime added to the quart. Keep moderately moist, over 65 degrees F., and

137

within 4 inches of the fluorescent tubes or in a partially sunny window. Use a balanced formula fertilizer.

* * * * * * * * * * * * * * * *

French Lavender is very much branched and has leaves with 1-inch narrow leaflets with the sides of each blade symmetrically and shallowly lobed. Touch the plant and the most delicious perfume is liberated. The usual outdoor Lavenders are much taller—this one grows to no more than 15 inches—and coarser. Accustomed to cool culture, they quickly succumb to house temperatures.

Perfumed plants are always acceptable gifts. All the more so with a Lavender that is still not as well known as it ought to be. With age it becomes woody and makes a handsome small shrub. This is the only state in which we would suggest that it be presented for major occasions. It takes about four years to reach this kind of maturity. On the other hand, small plants make excellent favors, hospitality gifts and subjects for the benefit sale table. We rate them intermediate to expert in culture.

The sawtooth leaves of this *Lavandula dentata* emit a heavenly scent when touched. Small pots make lovely hospitality gifts.

LEMON VINE. *Pereskia aculeata.* var. *godseffiana.*
All growers
All occasions
Cuttings

This is a plant of the cactus family with real leaves and branches that makes a fine pot or basket plant. It is one that can be handled by anyone from beginner to expert and will be enjoyed by all.

Pot in 2-1-1 soilless mix, replacing the perlite with sand. Allow to dry out between waterings, but not for more than a few days. Keep above 60 degrees F. and fertilize with a balanced formula. The addition of chelated iron can be beneficial. Plant color will be better in Full Sun, but it will grow well in Bright Reflected light or under fluorescent tubes at a distance of 4 inches. Cuttings root with surprising ease and speed. Just poke them into regular soilless mix, sphagnum moss or pure peat moss and keep just moist in a warm place with good light.

****

Pereskia aculeata is a strong-growing vine with fleshy, green, 2-inch leaves. The variety *godseffiana* is so different as to seem a separate plant. The stems grow much like rosebush canes but with more of a tendency to droop, which suits them for baskets. The leaves are 2 to 2½ inches long, oval-pointed and somewhat folded down the middle. New leaves are a bright pink-orange, turning to apricot as they age and eventually becoming green if not exposed to full light. This makes it a most colorful plant.

The Lemon Vine is now available from nurseries and by mail order. Still hardly known to indoor growers, it is destined to become a very popular plant.

The plant is quite fast growing and you can have a large basket plant within a year from a cutting. But even when the cutting is just rooted, the stiff-but-not-straight stem and the colorful leaves growing in a pleasing pattern make this a most attractive little plant. Small ones are just ideal for gifts and charity sales. Their very novelty will attract admiration and buyers. Large plants, which you can easily grow yourself, make regal gifts for a major occasion. For indoor gardeners, the Lemon Vine is truly one of the great discoveries of the last few years.

LOBELIA. *Lobelia erinus.*

Intermediates
Gifts, especially in winter
Seed

These lovely little plants with upright to trailing short stems and brilliant blue or white flowers make excellent winter pot plants. It is advisable to start with seed in the fall, strewing it on finely sieved potting mix and covering with a thin blanket of milled sphagnum moss. Place within 4 inches of the lamps and maintain a temperature of 70 to 80 degrees F. Keep moist at all times.

When the seedlings have four leaves, prick them out and transplant, putting four to six seedlings in a 4-inch shallow pot. Use a finely sieved 2-1-1 soilless mix with two tablespoons of powdered lime to the quart. Keep moist and fertilize with a high phosphate-potash formula. Place within 3 inches of the lamps. Lobelias do not like extreme heat, and a fan or air conditioning is advisable to prevent suffocation.

****

A plant as small as the garden Lobelia makes a show outdoors only when forming continuous strips as an edging. In the house, the changed scale of things makes the plant appear to be much bigger and more important. It is valuable especially for its brilliant blue color which is so rare in cultivated plants.

The Lobelia can be grown in pots or set in hanging pots or baskets. It looks particularly nice trailing from a small handcrafted clay pot with a fiber hanger. Thus, we have again a plant which is common enough in gardens but is a surprising gift in mid-winter and is a real gem that suggests spring in the worst period of weather.

MARIGOLD. *Tagetes.*

Beginners with fluorescent light
Party favors, hostess presents, benefits
Stem cuttings, seed

The very idea of propagating Marigolds from stem cuttings does not occur to the outdoor gardener because they are so easy to plant in the spring and, when they finish in the fall, seed is collected and the plants discarded. But if you watch the behavior of a Marigold a few days after a rain storm has beaten it down near the ground, you will notice that it puts out roots from the joints. That becomes useful when you bring them indoors in the fall and want to make winter gifts for friends.

Tall Marigolds look gawky indoors. It is the dwarf French and pom-

pom Marigolds that you must choose for indoor growing. Take these plants and make stem cuttings out of them, rooting them in ordinary potting soil with perlite added. Or, start fresh seed in September or later and have flowering plants right through the winter.

Indoors, these shallow-rooted plants need wide pots and a 2-1-1 soil-less mix with lime added. Sterilized garden soil with perlite will also do, but there is a greater risk of its drying out too quickly. Fertilize with a balanced formula at every watering and place the plants in a sunny window or within 3 inches of the fluorescent tubes. Window growing is unreliable because of cloudy days in winter. That is all there is to it! Marigolds of the kind mentioned bloom very well indoors with the temperature a normal 65 degrees F. or higher.

****

Marigolds are showy plants, yet ones we never see in winter in the shops because of the cost of growing them at that time of year and the inability of shops to maintain the needed temperature. The plants must be kept in bloom in order to sell, and only in the house can we provide adequate illumination to do the trick.

That is all the more reason why Marigolds are surprising and delightful gifts in winter. We would not suggest them as major presents, because they are relatively short-lived. But as young plants, they are ideal as party favors, as hostess presents and for benefit sales.

MICROSPERMA. *Eucnide bartonioides.*
Golden Tassel.
Intermediates
Small gifts
Seed

This is a small blooming plant no more than 9 inches high when in flower. The leaves are like those of the Piggy-back Plant—hairy and mapleish. Its flowers are 1½ inches, and bright yellow with many yellow stamens. It is a biennial that blooms the first season and will last a few months in a pot.

Use 2-1-1 soilless mix and keep moist at all times; if allowed to dry out, these plants will quickly succumb. Keep the temperature above 65 degrees F., and fertilize with a balanced formula. Grow within 4 inches of the fluorescent tubes. Propagation is from seed, with about 8 weeks to the first flowering. This is an intermediate plant.

****

This is a beautiful, relatively easy and little-known plant. Seed is carried by several mail-order firms. It makes a fine mid-winter small gift.

MING ARALIA. *Polyscias.*

Beginners
Home decoration, party favors, hospital present
Stem cuttings

These are magnificent foliage plants that are ornamental in every size from 4-inch pot plants to 4 footers in tubs. They are of easiest culture, so that any beginner can handle them. They deserve much greater popularity than they now enjoy.

Pot in 2-1-1 soilless mix and feed with a high nitrate formula. Keep in temperatures above 60 degrees F. and keep constantly moist. Light Shade or north light is sufficient and up to 15 inches under fluorescent tubes. Stem cuttings root in soilless mix without difficulty.

****

The most popular of the Polyscias is *P. fruticosa*, the Ming Aralia, also called the Parsley Aralia. It branches from a short, knobby, thick trunk with most of the growth being vertical. The stems are thin and flexible with many joints bearing leaves consisting of three leaflets that are very much divided like parsley.

A definite advantage of this plant is that cuttings always consist of a stem and closely packed leaves that give it a compact, bushy appearance from the start. Rooting is very quick and reliable. The plants grow quite rapidly and can be trained to any size without difficulty. When allowed to develop long stems, their irregular growth and the delicacy of the leaves lends them a decidedly oriental appearance. As large plants they are superb decorative plants for the living room.

These are most versatile plants that serve as gifts for any occasion, small or great. A large plant, for instance, is a worthy gift for a house-warming or an anniversary—or a wedding. Small plants make beautiful favors and benefit sales plants. When young plants are carefully trained for a few months and potted artistically, they have the appearance of works of art. An organization with a fund raising sale coming up might well purchase a big plant and cut up its many branches into cuttings. The stump will then grow even more beautifully with time.

P. filicifolia, the Fern Leaf Aralia, has deeper-cut, longer and more delicate leaflets, and the stems are even more contorted. It is a less sturdy plant. *P. quilfoylei* and *balfouriana* have more rounded leaflets that are usually variegated with white. They are less graceful, grow more slowly, and offer less material for cutting. But they are also lovely plants that can be grown in the same way as the Ming Aralia and make very fine presents for occasions of all kinds.

OXALIS REGNELLII.
Beginners, young people, specialist-hobbyists
Birthdays, favors, benefits
Division

This is probably the easiest of all flowering house plants and definitely within the capability of a beginner. That it is not more popular is astonishing. It grows from scaly, fleshy, thick roots that perform like a bulb or tuber. The stalks of the leaves, growing directly out of these roots, are up to 6 inches long. The leaf consists of three absolutely triangular leaflets, each about an inch from the broad base to the point of attachment. They're dark green on top and red below and fold down the middle of the leaf at night. Flower stalks grow just like the leaves and bear several small, five-petalled white flowers that open successively.

Pot in 2-1-1 soilless mix with 2 tablespoons lime to the quart and fertilize with a balanced formula. Keep above 60 degrees F. Never let the plant go dry. Seed is not usually produced and you are therefore dependent on plants. However, these spread rapidly and the roots can be broken up and potted separately. The plant will bloom even in a north window all year round and, of course, under fluorescent light.

****

All the other tuberous Oxalis that are so much advertised in the catalogs go dormant for long periods. *O. regnellii* does not—it is a true everblooming plant. It *will* go dormant if you allow it to dry out, hence the warning on this point. Also it can get mite. The cure is to remove all leaves and stems and spray the surface of the soil with House and Garden Raid. Keep moist and the roots will resprout promptly. In case of dormancy, you'll just have to wait it out.

This is a great one to get someone started with plants—a young person, for instance, on the occasion of a birthday. It is easy to produce many flowering plants for favors or for the benefit sale table. We would not recommend it as a super gift simply because it is a plain plant, but it is ideal for a hospitality gift, a housewarming or for a specialist-hobbyist who is too wrapped up in just one kind of plant.

POLKA DOT PLANT. *Hypoestes phyllostachya.*

Intermediates
Party favors, hospitality gifts, young people
Stem cuttings

The Polka Dot Plant has an upright growth with many heart-shaped, hairy leaves 2 to 3 inches long and sprinkled with bright pink dots. It grows rapidly and soon reaches its maximum height of about 20 inches. Stems grow from the spreading roots if they have room in the pot.

Plant in 2-1-1 soilless mix and give Bright Reflected or Partial Sun. Under the fluorescent lamps, keep within 4 inches of the lights. Unless the light is sufficiently intense, the plant may grow too fast and, with the joints spread far apart, will not appear as leafy and compact as it should.

Though it is tolerant of moisture, it is advisable to grow Hypoestes fairly dry. Use a balanced formula fertilizer with every watering. Cuttings with a few leaves root in soilless mix without a covering, provided the temperature is maintained over 65 degrees F. It is recommended for intermediate growers.

****

This is one of the plants that can be grown to a respectable size in six months or less. In that time you can have a foot high and 6- to 8-inch across, handsome foliage plant in a 4-inch pot.

The plant is at its best only for a few months, after which it loses leaves lower down on the stem and if trimmed constantly soon becomes bare and unsightly instead of continuing to put out branches.

Therefore, this is a plant to give or sell as a well-grown, rooted cutting or in its prime when it has bushed out. The latter condition can be speeded up by planting four cuttings to a 4- to 6-inch pot. Either way, however, it makes an excellent party plant or hospitality gift. We should mention here, too, that out-of-season growth makes for a more appreciated plant. You will see Polka Dot Plants in the stores in spring but not at other times of the year.

POMEGRANATE, DWARF. *Punica granatum nana.*

Experts
Major gifts, special housewarming
Stem cuttings, seed

The dwarf Pomegranate is the only one of our house plants producing both handsome flowers and an actual fruit—a pomegranate about 1½ inches in diameter with the usual red coloring and seeds you can use for planting. Seed is available from mail-order houses, but we are not sure

Fuchsia-like flowers are followed by a colorful fruit on this Dwarf Pomegranate, *Punica granatum nana*.

they are of the everblooming type. Our own plants come from nurseries. There are many different slight variations, this being a very old cultivated plant, so you may have to experiment a bit before you find the right kind.

Grow in 3-2-1 soilless mix without lime and feed with a high nitrate formula and extra chelated iron. Keep moist at all times and maintain the temperature over 65 degrees F. Plants are subject to mite attacks, usually in summer. Propagation is by stem cuttings. Seed germinates in 20 or more days. When the plants are quite young, start to trim in order to produce a branching plant. With age, Pomegranates can be trained into single-stemmed, attractive trees no more than 15 inches high.

****

As small plants, Pomegranates have little attraction, and must not be allowed to bloom until they are well-rooted and have the branches to bear the rather large flowers. These are somewhat like Fuchsias but with an orange calyx and tomato-red, silky petals that never unfold outward completely. Usually, fruit can be produced merely by blowing into the mature flower. Don't start more than one to a small tree or it will stop blooming.

A well-trained treelet is one of the finest of all house plant gifts. It can rarely be bought at nurseries or florists. With its many branches, small narrow leaves and flaming flowers and fruit, it is really a glorious plant for someone who will appreciate it and be able to take care of it. You will be safe in considering this a major present for any plant lover who has plants and experience.

PORTULACA. *Portulaca.*
Experts
Winter gifts, table favors
Stem cuttings

Portulaca is still another plant you can bring into the house in late summer, provided you have ones of a compact variety. It is such a sun lover that it is almost inconceivable as an indoor plant. Yet it does very well under fluorescent light in the depths of winter. Or, you can start it from seed from September on for winter bloom.

Plant seeds right in the pot in a mix of 1 part humus, 1 part sterilized garden soil or potting soil, and 2 parts sand. Four seeds will fit a 4-inch pot. It should be an azalea-type pot as Portulaca is very shallow-rooted. Once the seeds sprout, fertilize with a high phosphate-potash formula once a week and water sparingly, allowing the soil to dry out well in between waterings. They have quite succulent stems and will not suffer.

Keep the tops of the plants 2 to 3 inches below the lights at all times. A temperature above 65 degrees F. is advisable. If the seedlings elongate, pin their branches into the soil very carefully, for the flesh is tender and easily damaged. The young plants will root at the joints and gain added strength for blooming. Remove the first buds. The flowers last only a day; remove the dead ones promptly. If there is an excess of growth, cut it off and use it as stem cuttings. Rooting is easy. Plants from the garden, if a little weary after a summer of heavy blooming, should be denuded of branches which can be planted as cuttings for a fall-winter crop.

We recommend these plants to at least a moderately experienced grower because they need close attention and continuous grooming.

****

Few plants are more colorful for their size than Portulacas. Not only are the flowers quite large, but the coloring is vibrant and there is no end of variation in shades.

As with our other summer annuals, these make splendid winter gifts that are even more surprising than the others. But make sure that the recipients have fluorescent lights or a warm sun porch; winter sun at a windowsill is not sufficiently reliable to keep Portulacas blooming.

POTHOS. *Epipremnum aureum.*
Beginners
Benefits, housewarmings, shut-ins
Stem cuttings

Pothos are small trailing vines with heart-shaped leaves up to 4 inches long that, in the usual variety grown, called 'Marble Queen', are ivory or creamy-yellow colored, blotched with green and gray-green.

These are beginners' plants, and have largely replaced the small vining philodendrons on windowsills and in offices. Pot in 2-1-1 soilless mix, keep moderately moist and above 60 degrees F. Feed with a high nitrate formula. Pothos will grow in north light or up to 15 inches under the fluorescent tubes. Propagation is by stem cuttings which root in water or moist vermiculite.

****

Very commonly available in variety stores, Pothos is a gift only for someone who has very few plants. They can be inexpensive small pot plants for a benefit sale table.

Pothos is an ideal small house plant for a beginner.

PRAYER PLANT. *Maranta leuconeura.*
Intermediates
Important gifts, shower presents, housewarmings
Stem cuttings

Marantas are essentially prostrate plants whose angular stems consist mainly of the sheaths of the leaves. The latter are broadly oval, smooth and 3 to 5 inches long. At night the leaf blades fold upwards, giving rise to their common name. We consider them best for intermediate growers for, though they are easy to maintain for a while, they deteriorate if not treated properly.

Pot in 3-2-1 soilless mix and keep evenly moist. They do not like to be dried out. Fertilize with a high potash formula. Temperature should be kept above 65 degrees F. They will grow in north light, but do better in Bright Reflected or Partial Sun. They are quite happy under fluorescent lamps at a distance of 1 foot. Propagation is by stem cuttings in a covered box.

****

There are three principal varieties. Var. *leuconeura*, sometimes called Var. *massangeana*, is dark gray with gray veins and silvery-gray featherings. Var. *kerchoveana* is light green with four to six distinct brownish-green blotches on either side of the mid-rib in a straight line. Var. *erythroneura* has rosy-red veining with the veins very prominent. *Leuconeura* and *kerchoveana* are easiest; *erythroneura* is a bit more tempermental.

The problem with the Marantas is that they are shallow-rooted and for some reason seem to exhaust their soil after six to nine months. Repotting in fresh soil usually rejuvenates the plant. But it is fast growing and the stems root easily.

Small pots of the Prayer Plant are common enough in the shops, but well-grown baskets are more unusual and far more beautiful. Growing a good-looking plant is not difficult and can be accomplished from a single stem in six months or less. The plants have a tendency to grow toward the light so that indoors it is advisable to turn them around occasionally in order to equalize their growth. They are sensitive to drops in temperature and over-watering at that time.

Good-looking small baskets of Marantas make very acceptable gifts and, if you can grow a large one of *M. erythroneura*, it is a special present indeed, worthy of an important occasion.

VELVET PLANT, THE PURPLE.
Gynura aurantiaca.

Beginners
Housewarmings, shower gifts, table favors
Stem cuttings

We can't think of another Daisy family plant with more spectacular foliage. It is really a vine and is usually grown in a basket, its oval-pointed, 3-inch leaves (purple-red below and green above) alternately lining the long trailing stems. The whole leaf is very hairy and, when the plant is exposed to bright light, the hairs on the upper surface also turn bright purple-red and quite hide the green surface.

Pot in 1-1-1 soilless mix and keep moist at all times. For best results, hang it in a sunny window. It will also grow well under the fluorescent tubes. Fertilize with a high nitrate formula. This is a tropical plant and requires a temperature of 65 degrees F. or better, but it is not fussy about humidity. Cuttings take readily in the moistened mix.

****

Gynuras are fine gift plants, either as large baskets or as small pot plants. A very rapid rate of growth makes it easy to have a big, showy basket rather quickly. But it is also very attractive with a single rooted cutting to a small pot. Make the cutting branch a bit by nipping the first new growths. It will then grow as a very compact mass of color as long as it is not given a larger pot.

The Purple Velvet Plant, *Gynura aurantiaca*, is the most colorful of foliage basket plants—and easy to grow. Give it to a beginner or propagate many cuttings for a plant sale.

RIBBON BUSH. *Homalocladium platycladum.*

Beginners
Hospitality gifts, benefits
Stem cuttings

This is a strangely attractive shrubby plant that any beginner can handle. It has round woody stems, but the branches are like stiff green ribbons and bear arrowhead-shaped leaves an inch long. In winter it usually loses the leaves but looks not much worse for the experience.

Grow in sterilized garden soil with perlite added or in 1-1-1 soilless mix. Fertilize sparingly with a high nitrate formula. Keep evenly moist in summer but rather dry in winter. The plant will suffer if the temperature goes much below 65 degrees F. It will grow in a north window or under fluorescent light. With time, it becomes a 2-foot-high plant with many branches, even when badly underpotted.

Propagation is by means of the branches, which it produces in great quantity so that there is always plenty of cutting material.

★★★★★★★★★★★★★★★★

The novelty of the plant makes it a pleasant gift for any occasion. Since few people know it well and its appearance is so unusual, it is a pretty surefire offering even though it has no apparent beauty of color or form. Because of these qualities and its trouble-free culture, we have found it popular with all those who become acquainted with it.

ROSE, MINIATURE.

Experts
Gifts
Not recommended for propagation

Because we admire them as much as anyone and are sure that many readers would wonder at the absence of these plants from our pages, we feel that we have to comment on them.

The best amateur grower of miniature roses that we know has to admit that his plants go out-of-doors in summer and that he uses a pesticide not generally available to the public to keep spider mites at bay. Not a single one of our many friends who are experts in indoor growing has been consistently successful with these plants. Finally, except for the patient and knowledgeable, propagation is not easy. Or we should say, rather, that the plants do take root without too much difficulty, but usually succumb to fungus or mite attack before they can develop reserve energy.

150

For these reasons, we consider miniature roses delightful plants to buy as gifts for friends and we can understand anyone appreciating their charm and being satisfied with a few weeks of healthy bloom. But we believe that that is about all there is to be gained from them at the present time.

Miniature roses make charming gifts. But the recipient will have to keep the spider mites at bay.

ROSEMARY. *Rosmarinus officinale.*

Intermediates, experts
Shower favors, hospital presents, gourmet party favors
Seed, stem cuttings

Rosemary is a shrubby plant with extremely narrow leaves under 1 inch long. It is the most aromatic of the herbs and useful in soups and meat dishes. It is also one of the easiest of the herbs to grow and very long lasting. We have seen plants in greenhouses that were at least 30 years old.

Pot in 1-1-1 soilless mix with 4 tablespoons of lime chips to the quart. Keep rather potbound. Water daily unless the temperature goes below 60 degrees F. The pot must *never* dry out for more than a few hours. Formerly the direction always was—allow to dry out between waterings. This is *totally false* in the house and will result in the death of the plant. Fertilize with a high nitrate formula.

Rosemary can grow in quite low light, but the many branches will elongate. Better form is achieved through exposing them in the brightest location you have. They do fine under fluorescent lamps, 3 to 4 inches below the tubes.

Cuttings root moderately easily in a closed box with vermiculite. They will get fungus if the vermiculite is too wet. Seeds germinate well and need to be kept moist, over 75 degrees F. until leaves are formed, and within 1 or 2 inches of the fluorescent tubes.

****

A most versatile gift plant, Rosemary is planted here in a chunk of feather rock. It's easy to grow and very long lasting.

A difficult problem with Rosemary is picking the right kind of plant. There are numerous fine differences in habit and the set of the leaves. Those that look best in a nursery pot are not necessarily ideal for trimming, having been grown too fast. Also, you want a plant that develops a good trunk and will tolerate warm house temperatures. We recommend the more upright types rather than the prostrate ones. Start with seed or, better still, with a well-rooted plant that already has a trunk. Repot promptly in soilless mix, but remove only excess old soil around the roots in doing so, or you may harm it. Regular trimming improves the appearance and strengthens the trunk.

Small Rosemary plants are fine for small gifts, but their chief virtue is that they can be trained in about a year into a fine bonsai appearance. Few plants are more amenable to this treatment. The woodiness, the regular branching and the needle-like leaves make this possible. Presented in a suitably attractive pot, nothing could be finer.

SELAGINELLA UNCINATA. Peacock Selaginella.

Beginner with terrarium
Terrarium gifts for the ill, favors, hospitality gifts
Stem cuttings

Selaginellas are very primitive plants. They have spreading branches lined with the tiniest leaves, giving them a feathery effect. Some grow as much as 2 feet high while others stay quite low, but all require terrarium conditions of high humidity. Our favorite species is *Selaginella uncinata*, the Peacock Selaginella, so-called because its leaves are an iridescent blue. There are few foliage plants more elegant in form and color.

The plant will grow in any transparent container with cover, in soilless mix or sphagnum moss. The soil is never fertilized and should be kept in a just-barely-moist condition. The temperature should at all times be above 60 degrees F. Very little light is needed. The plant can grow in Light Shade away from a window or up to 2 feet below fluorescent tubes.

A sprig of Selaginella laid on top of soil will soon root itself with these conditions. It will spread inside a small terrarium, some branches standing upright, others crawling along the soil, and some attaching themselves by roots that develop at every joint. If there is no excess moisture in the soil and the top is kept closed, the plant can easily go for well over a year without any attention at all. Don't open the top except to take cuttings to start other plants.

****

The care-free culture of this plant makes it an ideal gift for the ill who cannot take care of a plant or for the over-busy or lazy grower. For small gifts, snifters with fitted tops or round bowls of glass are ideal. They can be of any size, from 3 or 4 inches to 10 inches in diameter. Inside a clear glass bottle, the plant will grow happily. As long as it is visible through the glass, this too makes a fine gift. As favors, for hospitality gifts and at benefit sale tables, this novelty will be equally successful.

If you wish to grow great numbers of plants, give your starting plant more light and it will grow quite rapidly.

SINNINGIA, MINI. *Sinningia.*
Intermediates, experts, specialist-hobbyists
Gift terrariums, benefits, important gifts
Seed, tuber offsets

Seed of the mini-Sinningias is now available. Long the delight of hobbyists, these admirable little plants can now be grown by anybody who has fair intermediate skill and experience with house plants. They are tuberous, with 1- to 2½-inch tube flowers flaring into five lobes, borne on thin upright stems. The leaves are quite flat, so total height even in bloom is no more than 3 or 4 inches. They are suitable for 2- to 3-inch pots.

They require 2-1-1 soilless mix with 2 tablespoons of lime chips or crushed eggshell to the quart. Culture is, in other respects, almost the same as that of African Violets. But we'll repeat that they need 65 degrees F. temperature, constant moisture without sogginess, regular fertilizing with a high phosphate-potash formula, and a position in Partial Sun or 4 to 12 inches under the lamps. Because the seed is usually a mixed lot, the plants will vary in their need for light.

Propagate by tuber offsets and by using the extra shoots that grow from the tubers as cuttings. Most of the plants will produce seed spontaneously. With some of the seed plants, the tubers will go dormant while in others they are nearly everblooming. High humidity is very helpful for flowering and all of these plants do well in terrarium conditions.

★★★★★★★★★★★★★★★★

The colors of the flowers range from pink to purple-blue. Seed collections usually include the variety 'Cindy-Ella', with its beautiful trumpet flowers, purple on top with a white lip and throat speckled with purple. This and other kinds, such as the famous 'Doll Baby', 'Pink Petite', 'Stuck-up', 'Freckles', 'Wood Nymph' and *Sinningia pusilla* are sold by the nurseries as plants. There are many others, all equally enticing.

Although all of these are small plants, they are relatively important gifts because they have been known primarily only to hobby-specialists

154

until now. In every situation where a small plant can be given to someone with a little skill in growing, these are delightful presents. When they are planted in little terrariums, their perky flowers are adorable and they will need little or no attention for a long time. For the benefit sale table, a terrarium setting makes these little plants very profitable, for there are few who can resist them in bloom.

SPIDER PLANT. *Chlorophytum.*

Beginners
Shower gifts, housewarmings
Stem cuttings

Spider plants are among the very easiest plants to grow as they need little light and can be watered irregularly. They rarely, if ever, have pests or diseases.

The plants grow rapidly by shallow underground roots that send up tufts of leaves. To encourage spreading growth for propagation, they should be planted in broad, shallow pots or baskets. At almost any time of year the plant also puts out long bare stems that develop plantlets and

Easy and popular, the variegated Spider Plant is a wonderful gift for anyone just beginning a plant collection.

little white flowers at the tips. These tips can be pinned down and rooted in the soil of the pot. When the central plant has put up enough tufts to fill a pot, you can divide it by simply cutting the connecting piece of root. These plants can be potted up and will start growing immediately.

Ordinary sterilized garden soil will suit the plants. But if you wish to get quick growth, use 2-1-1 soilless mix and fertilize with a high nitrate formula, watering regularly. More flower stalks are produced in low than high light, so keep your plant in Bright Reflected light or Light Shade. Placement in a north window will also do.

****

For gifts, Spider Plants are among the easiest to multiply, but they suffer from the disadvantage of being so very common. However, there are numerous variations and, if you can get a cutting or buy a plant with a particularly handsome white and green striping, and can then grow good-sized baskets, they will be much appreciated by those who have little experience but a hunger for greenery. Some of the newer variations have rather broader, shorter leaves with plenty of white, and are more ornamental than most.

STRAWBERRY BEGONIA. *Saxifraga stolonifera.*

Intermediates
Party favors, young people, birthdays
Rooting stolons

Strawberry Begonias are a propagator's dream plants because of their profuse production of stolons with plantlets at the tips. Place the parent plant in the middle of a ring of small pots filled with soil and pin down the stolon tips with hair pins. In next to no time, you will have flourishing little plants.

They are charming basket plants consisting of clusters of kidney-shaped leaves veined with silver on hairy red stalks. Give them 2-1-1 soilless mix with 4 tablespoons of lime chips to the quart. Substituting sand for the perlite is even better. The roots are not deep, but the spreading habit of the plant requires shallow but broad pots. Rather cool growing, they should be protected against the summer heat waves. A temperature range of 55 to 80 degrees F. is best. Keep moderately moist at all times and fertilize with a high phosphate-potash formula. Keep on the dry side in winter. They prefer Partial Sun or Bright Reflected light and will do well suspended under fluorescent tubes at a distance of 4 inches.

****

Although seen in the shops from time to time, Strawberry Begonias are not very common in spite of almost everyone being familiar with the name of the plant. For this reason, they make welcome gifts for modest occasions and are perfect for place setting favors.

TROPICAL FRUIT SEEDS

A number of tropical fruits that appear seasonally in the shops yield seeds that can be grown with ease into handsome small trees that are long-lived and undemanding. The best known example is the Avocado, which has become the beginner's plant par excellence.

We do not list orange, lemon or dates because the fruiting varieties on the market are not the best plants for the house. You will do far better with plants of the hybridized dwarf lemons and oranges. The house plant date tree is *Phoenix roebelinii*, a dwarf species. All three are slow growers and difficult to prepare as gifts.

The seed of all the fruits we do list are available from seedsmen. When you get their catalogs, look for other interesting tropical bushes and trees. Many of these can be rewarding and make attractive gift plants.

AVOCADO. *Persea americana.*
Beginners
Housewarmings, all occasions
Seed

The Avocado is so familiar that discussion would seem superfluous. However, there is one matter that galls us. In order to write articles and books on this plant, it has been considered necessary to invent all kinds of complications in germinating the seed and growing it, when nothing could be simpler.

The Avocado pit is an over-sized seed with enough food storage to grow a sizable plant without soil. Any special precautions in handling it are altogether unnecessary. All you have to do is bury the seed with just its top projecting from 2-1-1 soilless mix. Keep it moist, warm and in bright light. It will germinate promptly. The intensity of light is important only because it affects the length of the first shoot before it forms leaves. The shoot can be kept short by giving the seedling the best light you have.

The only other suggestion is to trim early and often in order to avoid a tall, leggy plant. You can't start, though, until there are at least three pairs of real leaves. Then nip the new growth. As branches lengthen and rebranch, keep them under control by frequent trimming. Moderate moisture, a temperature over 65 degrees F. and a high nitrate fertilizer with trace elements encourage good growth. The leaves are subject to mite, mealybug and scale infestation.

ANNATTO. *Bixa orellana.*
Intermediates, experts
Hospitality gifts, benefits, party favors
Seed

Strictly speaking, Bixa doesn't belong in this group since it does not produce an edible fruit. We include it here because it is in a category of its own and does not belong with our other, more common plants—since few people are growing it as yet.

Annatto seed can be bought in glass bottles at Puerto Rican stores in metropolitan areas and in chain groceries or from mail-order herb and spice seedsmen. It is a red seed that, when heated in oil, gives out red coloring matter. This is used as a substitute for saffron as a coloring for rice by the peoples of the Caribbean islands. In our experience, the seed in the bottles germinates readily in the usual way.

Indoors, the tree is slow growing, much-branched, and bears heart-shaped leaves 2 to 3 inches long. It requires 2-1-1 soilless mix, a high nitrate fertilizer and Partial Sun or fluorescent light. Keep moderately moist. Temperatures should be above 65 degrees F. at all times. Our two-year-old plants are kept trimmed to no more than a foot high but are well formed.

JUJUBE. *Ziziphus jujuba.* Chinese Date.
Intermediates, experts
Friendship gifts, dinner party favors, benefits
Seed

The Chinese Date is a pretty little tree like a small cherry with 2-inch narrow leaves. The fruit is oval, about an inch long and bright red. When dried, it has much the texture and flavor of a date. The dried fruit is sold in packages in oriental stores. You will find it quite palatable, and it makes a delicious dessert when stewed with sugar and a piece of vanilla bean.

Remove the soft parts from the seed and nick the side with a file. Plant in 1-1-1 soilless mix. Germination may take a month or more. When the seedling is well up, transplant it to a pot and as soon as it has a few leaves, start to trim. Keep rather cool if possible, for it likes a tempera-ture between 50 and 80 degrees F. An air-conditioned home is ideal.

Fertilize with a high nitrate formula with trace elements. Water sparingly but regularly. Keep in Full or Partial Sun or under fluorescent tubes.

MANGO. *Mangifera indica.*
Beginners, intermediates
Birthdays, hospitality gifts
Seed

With its 6-inch, narrow, oval-pointed leaves, shiny dark green and somewhat leathery, the Mango is typical of many large tropical trees. The fruit is on the market from August to October. The best kind is about 6 inches long with a bright yellow and red skin. The small yellow fruits and very green ones (even if they ripen red) may be virused or immature.

Eat the delicious fruit and save the seed, which is thin and 2½ to 3 inches long. Dry in the air for a few hours until the thin, tough skin is partly dry. With a sharp knife, slice the skin and remove the inner lima bean-like seed. Plant in a pot filled with 2-1-1 soilless mix, setting the sprouting top just above soil level. The sprout is just where it would be on a bean seed, on the broader top of the thin side.

Germination is very quick at 75 to 80 degrees F. in reflected light or at the end of the fluorescent tubes—not in bright light. Single seeds often produce several shoots, making a bushy plant immediately. When the stems are single, trim them like you do an Avocado and grow in the same conditions. Move to Partial Sun or the center of the fluorescent fixture after the plant has several leaves. New leaves grow out pale-colored and very limp, but soon gain substance and dark green color. If the tree is kept under-potted, it can be maintained no more than a foot or two high. In a larger pot it will take off.

SPANISH LIME. *Melicoccus bijugatus.*
Beginners, intermediates
Housewarmings, shower gifts, anniversaries
Seed

We have seen Spanish Limes, or Genips, on the market in both the spring and fall. They are nearly round, green fruit about an inch in diameter and come clustered on a branch about a foot long. The surface is dull green and leathery-looking, but it easily splits and you can enjoy the sour-sweet taste of the gummy flesh that covers the one large, round, ivory-colored seed.

Remove the pulp from the seed and file a small hole on the side down to the meat. Soak overnight in water and plant the following day in a Jiffy 7 so that the top is covered. Keep moist and at 75 degrees F. or higher until germination, which is usually within three weeks. Then pot up in 2-1-1 soilless mix and feed with a high nitrate fertilizer. Moderate moisture is best, but once the plant is partly grown it is quite drought resistant.

This is a handsome plant with compound leaves in pairs and the stalks winged. Pruning is necessary at an early stage or it will take off and grow a cane 10 feet high or more. Trimmed, it stays small and will branch. This is a splendid novelty that is an easy and enduring gift.

ST. JOHN'S BREAD. *Ceratonia siliqua.*
Intermediates
Hospitality gifts, birthdays
Seed

St. John's Bread's long, locust-like beans are sold in the dried state in Hispanic and Puerto Rican vegetable stores and groceries. Remove the beans, file and plant just like Spanish Lime. The tree, with somewhat shorter, shinier leaves, is similar in appearance to the Avocado but more compact and closer-leaved. Grow just like an Avocado.

STAR FRUIT. *Averrhoa carambola.*
Intermediates, experts
Hospitality gifts, birthdays
Seed

These soft, oval, yellow fruits that are star-like in cross-section appear in the markets for a short period in the fall each year. Save the seeds, which are quite small, and treat like Annatto.

The little tree is particularly charming. What appear to be branches are actually compound leaves consisting of many opposite leaflets.

TAMARIND. *Tamarindus indica.*

Beginners, intermediates
Benefits, dinner party favors, young people
Seed

Tamarind beans, fatter and narrower than St. John's Bread, are sometimes available in dried form in the markets. Recently, the individual seeds with their thick gummy covering have been packed in plastic bags. In the Caribbean, the seeds are soaked and strained through a sieve. The resulting liquid sweetened with sugar is a tartly-sweet, very refreshing beverage. In India, where the Tamarind is native, a concentrate is packed in jars. This can be bought here in Indian grocery stores. A teaspoon mixed with water and sugar makes this wonderful drink.

When you get one of the packs, soak the seeds for three or four days. Then the seed can be pressed out clean with your fingers. Follow the same procedure with seeds extracted from beans.

Plant in Jiffy 7's or 2-1-1 soilless mix. Keep moist and warm. Germination usually follows in two or three weeks. Place under fluorescent light or Bright Reflected sunlight and maintain at over 65 degrees F. Fertilize with a high nitrate formula and keep moist at all times.

The tree has a cinnamon-colored trunk, numerous branches and compound leaves consisting of ½-inch oblong leaflets. Most people take it for a Mimosa on first sight. We have grown an 8-footer in a couple of years. But, if kept in a small pot and trimmed well, it will spread out in a most graceful manner. Of all the tropical treelets, this is our favorite.

Source List

WHERE TO BUY SEED

Arndt's Floral Garden, Troutdale, OR 97060. List 25¢.

Brudy, John, P.O.B. 1348, Cocoa Beach, FL 32931. Exotic plant seeds.

Burgess Seed and Plant Co., Galesburg, MI 49053.

Burpee, W. Atlee, Co., Philadelphia, PA 19132.

Deedees, Box 416, Menlo Park, CA 94025.

Dow Seeds Hawaii Ltd., P.O.B. 30144, Honolulu, HI 96820.

Exotica Seeds, 820 S. Lorraine Blvd., Los Angeles, CA 90005. List 25¢.

Gurney Seed & Nursery Co., Yankton, SD 57078.

Hudson, J.L., P.O.B. 1058, Redwood City, CA 94064. Catalog $1.00. Big list of tropical and garden plants.

Hurov's Tropical Seeds, P.O.B. 10387, Honolulu, HI 96816.

Park, Geo. W., Seed Co., Greenwood, SC 29646. Catalog.

Thompson & Morgan, 401 Kennedy Blvd., Somerdale, NJ 08083. Catalog $1.00.

World Seed Service, Box 01058, Redwood City, CA 94064. Catalog 50¢.

MAIL ORDER HOUSE PLANTS

Alberts & Merkel Bros., Inc., 2210 S. Federal Hwy., Boynton Beach, FL 33435. Outstanding list of foliage plants.

Arant's Exotic Greenhouses, Rt. 3, Box 972, Bessemer, AL 35020. Catalog $1.50. Gesneriads, foliage plants and many others. Our experience is that catalog listings are often not available here.

Barrington Greenhouses, 860 Clements Rd., Barrington, NJ 08016.

Bolduc's Greenhill Nursery, 2131 Vallejo Street, St. Helena, CA 94574. Ferns.

Buell's Greenhouses, Eastford, CT 06242. Gesneriads, especially Gloxinias.

Burgess Seed and Plant Company, 67 Battle Creek Street, Galesburg, MI 49053.

Edelweiss Gardens, Box 66, Robbinsville, NJ 08691. List 50¢.

Fennell Orchid Company, 26717 S.W. 157 Avenue, Homestead, FL 33030. Orchids and exotic foliage plants.

Garden Nook, The, Highway No. 1, Raleigh, NC 27614.

Glasshouse Works, Stewart, OH 45778.

Goochland Nurseries, Inc., Pembroke, FL 33866. Plant list.

Greenland Flower Shop, Port Matilda, PA 16870. Catalog 50¢.

Henrietta's Nursery, 1345 North Brawley Avenue, Fresno, CA 93705. Catalog $1.00. Cacti and succulents.

Hewston Green, P.O.B. 3115, Seattle, WA 98114. Catalog 50¢. Interesting list.

International Growers Exchange, Box 397, Farmington, MI 48024. Catalog $2.00.

Kartuz Greenhouses, 92 Chestnut St., Wilmington, MA 01887. Catalog 50¢. Tops in gesneriads, also begonias.

Lauray of Salisbury, Undermountain Rd., Salisbury, CT 06068. Catalog 50¢. Miscellaneous house plants, especially gesneriads, cacti and succulents. First class.

Logee's Greenhouses, Danielson, CT 06239. Catalog $2.00.

Loyce's Flowers, Rt. 2, Granbury, TX 76048. Large list. Hoyas and Bougainvilleas.

Lyndon Lyon, 14 Mutchler St., Dolgeville, NY 13329. Gesneriads.

McComb's Greenhouses, New Straitsville, OH 43776. Varied catalog with many interesting items.

Mellinger's Inc., 2310 West South Range, North Lima, OH 44452. Catalog contains varied list of seeds and plants.

Morrison, Pat/Heffner, Jim, 5305 S.W. Hamilton St., Portland, OR 97221. Outstanding for gesneriads, begonias and other house plants.

Park, Geo. W., Seed Co., Greenwood, SC 29647. Catalog.

Plant Room, The, 7373 Trafalgar Road, Hornby, Ontario, CANADA. List. Miscellaneous house plants.

Sunnybrook Farms Nursery, 9448 Mayfield Rd., Chesterland, OH 44026. Catalog 50¢. Fine herb list and others.

Tropical Plants, Box 2186, Harlingen, TX 78550. Catalog $2.00.

World Gardens, 845 Pacific Avenue, Willows, CA 95988. Catalog 50¢.

WHERE TO BUY SUPPLIES

Burpee, W. Atlee, Co., Philadelphia, PA 19132.

Calico Leather Company, 2402 Glassell, Orange, CA 92665. Planters, baskets, hangers.

Ceramics International Inc., 625 Broadway, San Diego, CA 92101. Pottery containers.

Consolidated Art Industries, 4411 Staunton Avenue, Los Angeles, CA 90058. Plastic and redwood planters. Hangers.

Dode's Gardens, 1490 Saturn Street, Merritt Island, FL 32952. House plant supplies.

Fleco Industries, 3347 Halifax, Dallas, TX 75247. Plant stands with fluorescent lights.

Flora Greenhouses, Box 1191, Burlingame, CA 94010. Plant stands with fluorescent lights.

Floralite Company, 4124 East Oakwood Rd., Oak Creek, WI 53154. Light garden equipment.

Gone to Pot Nursery & Supply Co., 6310 Chicago Avenue, Pensacola, FL 32508.

Grass Roots Ltd., 8 Crestview, Bloomfield, CT 06002. House plant supplies.

Green House, The, 9515 Flower Street, Bellflower, CA 90706. Plant stands with fluorescent lights.

Greeson, Bernard D., 3548 N. Cramer, Milwaukee, WI 53211. House plant supplies.

H.P. Supplies, 16337 Wayne Rd., Livonia, MI 48154.

House Plant Corner, The, Box 5000, Cambridge, MD 21613. House plant supplies. Catalog 50¢.

Indoor Gardening Supplies, P.O. Box 40567, Detroit, MI 48240.

International Register Co., Spring Grove, IL 60081. Timers.

Light Garden, The, Brewster, MA 02631. Plants, supplies.

Mary's African Violets, 19788 San Juan, Detroit, MI 48221. Excellent for house plant supplies.

Mellinger's, North Lima, OH 44452. Extensive catalog.

Mosser Lee Co., Millston, WI 54623. Peat and sphagnum moss.

Paragon Electric Co., Two Rivers, WI 54241. Excellent timers.

Park, Geo. W., Seed Co., Inc., Greenwood, SC 29646. Miscellaneous supplies.

Patio Products, Inc., 2522 State Road, Cornwells Heights, PA 19020. Hangers, planters, terrariums.

Peters, Robert W., Inc., 2833 Pennsylvania St., Allentown, PA 18104. Fertilizers.

Public Service Lamp Corp., 410 West 16th Street, New York, NY 10011. *Wonderlite Mercury-Vapor Lamps.*

Schultz Company, 11730 Northline St., St. Louis, MO 63043. Liquid fertilizer.

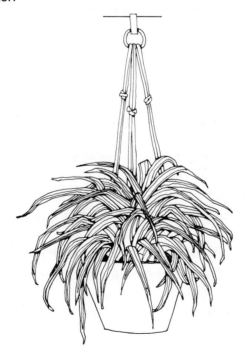

Shoplite Co., 566 Franklin Avenue, Nutley, NJ 07110. Stands with fluorescent lights and other equipment.

Sponge-Rok Sales, 7112 Hubbard Avenue, Middleton, WI 53562. Perlite.

Tropical Plant Products Inc., 1715 Silver Star Road, Orlando, FL 32804. Osmunda, tree fern and other tropical plant supplies.

Tube Craft Inc., 1311 W. 80th Street, Cleveland, OH 44102. Stands with fluorescent lights.

Verilux Inc., 35 Mason Street, Greenwich, CT 06830. *Verilux Tru-Bloom* lamps.

Volkmann Bros. Greenhouses, 2714 Minert St., Dallas, TX 75219. House plant supplies.

Walkers, The, Box 150, Luling, TX 78648. Pots.

PLANT SOCIETIES

All the plant societies have various services—bulletins or magazines, seed funds, opportunities to buy plants not readily available elsewhere. Write for details regarding dues, etc.

African Violet Society of America, Inc., P.O. Box 1326, Knoxville, TN 37901.

American Begonia Society, 6333 West 64th Place, Los Angeles, CA 90045.

The American Bonsai Society, 953 South Shore Drive—Lake Wakomis, Parkville, MO 64151.

American Fern Society, c/o LeRoy K. Henry, Carnegie Museum, Pittsburgh, PA 15213.

American Gesneriad Society, Worldway Postal Center, Box 91192, Los Angeles, CA 90009.

American Orchid Society, Botanical Museum of Harvard University, Cambridge, MA 02138.

American Gloxinia & Gesneriad Society, Inc., Eastford, CT 06242.

Bonsai Clubs International, 2354 Lida Dr., Mountain View, CA 90403.

Bromeliad Society Inc., P.O. Box 3279, Santa Monica, CA 90403.

Cactus & Succulent Society of America, Inc., Box 167, Reseda, CA 91335.

Herb Society of America, 300 Massachusetts Ave., Boston, MA 02115.

Indoor Light Gardening Society of America, c/o The Horticultural Society of New York, Inc., 128 West 58th St., New York, NY 10019.

International Geranium Society, 11960 Pascal Avenue, Colton, CA 92324.

Palm Society, 7229 S.W. 54th Ave., Miami, FL 33143.

Index

Adiantum, 125
African Violet, 23
  Honor Roll, 100
  Magazine, 100
African Violets, 12, 13, 16, 53, 72, 99-100
Aglaonema commutatum, 112; *costatum*, 113
Air conditioning, 40-41
Allamanda, 60
Alternanthera ficoidea (bettzickiana), 111-112
Aluminum Plant, 101-102
Annatto, 158
Anniversary gifts, 17-18
Artificial light, 33-37
Aspidistra, 3
Asplenium, 53
Averrhoa carambola, 160
Azaleas, 17, 60

Baby's Tears, 53
Ballast, 34
Balsam, 102-103
Basil, French, 103-104
Beginner plants, 9-10
Begonia, 12, 13, Calla Lily, 107; Fibrous rooted, 104-5; Rex, 106;
  Wax, 107
Begonia, Strawberry, 156-157
Benefit plants, 24-25; sales, 7
Bird cages, 92
Birthday plants, 17-18
Bixa orellana, 158
Black Leaf 40, 47
Bottle gardens, 49
Bromeliads, 12
Busy Lizzy, 132-133
Buying seeds and plants, 27-30

Cache-pots, 82-83
  ceramic, 87